Source's ʟ

MW01489658

YOUR

HIGHER

VISION

Patti Intoranat

TABLE OF CONTENTS

~Acknowledgements ~

The purpose of this book is to show readers how to see through the eyes of the higher vision of the Higher Self, from the point of view of the loving heart. The information in this book will demonstrate how to raise our perception from the ego to the Higher Self. This book shares the synchronicity of Patti's path of love to this point in her life. It contains the wisdom of how to be and become conscious of the Higher Self, Divine Source already within us. Once we come to this realization within us, we get to do less and be more. Source wanted Patti to write using her expression and her life story to reach people, by showing how she overcame life's obstacles and evolved through them.

This book is like an exquisite painting. Source/The Creator is the creative loving painter. Patti is the beautiful painting (the storyteller). Scot is the skillful framer of the painting (the editor). The meaning of the painting is more than just the picture. Just like being inspired by great art, each person will be affected in their own way from the experience. The wisdom gained from this book is what you learn about yourself and the increase in awareness of your mind, your Higher Self, and your own connection to Divine Source.

This book will help readers innerstand the power of divine love within all of us, assist everyone to claim it, and be empowered by it. Patti has been trusting the guidance from the Divine Source/the Higher Self, the source of knowledge, the most loving and pure light, guiding her through her own evolution. She is committed to be of service to others, taking this opportunity to help shine this guiding light to all who seek it.

The book includes Patti sharing her own personal story about her miraculous experience of self-healing and several stories of people who Patti served as a facilitator supporting them in their self-healing. During these sessions there were messages from peoples' Higher Selves that touched Patti's heart and helped her in her own evolution. With Patti's purest intention, she wishes to share these amazing gifts of knowledge with everyone.

While Patti was working on her last revisions of this book, the Covid-19 Pandemic was taking place. Patti utterly believes that the guidance from the Source of knowledge in this book is needed more than ever. Please read this book with an open heart and mind. See and feel what information you resonate with and allow it to help you in the circumstances you are in. Utilize the knowledge you receive to its highest potential to assist you with is this time of needs and beyond.

~In Loving Gratitude~

I would like to express my heartfelt gratitude to Source for pure unconditional love and guidance, leading me through this entire journey. To the late Dolores Cannon for her love and knowledge, and to her family for their dedication in carrying on her legacy. To my fellow practitioners who are dedicated to Dolores' method and utilize it to serve humanity. To all the teachers who have taught me throughout this amazing journey. To all the clients who believe in our work and for giving us their support.

To Sue Gallagher for being a dear friend and allowing herself to be a bridge between Source and I, and to help us experience Oneness, the experience that helps me learn many lessons about how to surrender more fully to unconditional love. To Scot Holliday for his genuine friendship, kindred spirit and help in perfecting this book, and for fanning Source's flames to burn brighter and more intensely, bringing the painting to life. To Steve Conn for being a friend for life and for his love for the purpose and message of this book. To Leela Vosko for offering her expertise so this treasure can be found by many. To Mike Trevisan, Janet Tingley and Lydia Foley for their kindred spirits, ongoing support, pure intention and the loyal friendships which are rare to find. To my family for their love and support and continuous belief in her. We are on this journey together. To Narisa and Art, for their talents and their contributions. To the readers who read this book, accepting this book with an open mind and open heart. To all the souls who are here at this time to experience history in the making, during the great ascension of our planet earth, Gaia and humanity to a new frequency, moving us from an ego mind-based reality to one based on love and divinity.

~Preface by Scot Holliday ~

This book tells the story of Patti's life, how she shifted from duality to oneness — overcoming her lower self, her feelings, her fears, her experiences of how she put together the pieces of her life and was able to shift her consciousness "to be", living aligned to the Higher Self, the loving heart. A large part of this story is how she became a Level Three Quantum Healing Hypnosis Technique (QHHT) Practitioner, and her experiences helping others claim their own authentic truth. This is just the surface of the story.

This book contains energetic transmissions that activate your awareness and increase your consciousness. When you read the stories within this book, it is like downloading software to your personal computer (the consciousness), allowing you to create a new way of being. When I started giving Patti the support to help her with this book in December 2019, my consciousness was heightened. I became more tuned into my heart, my Higher Self and the alignment of my own heart to Divine Source. My ability to imagine and create more of the life I have been seeking was heightened. I decided to apply that increased awareness to support this book in being the best it can possibly be at inspiring and teaching others to connect with their own heart, Higher Self and live at their highest vibration.

This book will give the reader a step-by-step explanation of how to connect to love and your own Higher Self and live the life of your dreams. This book shares frequencies of what love, connecting to the Higher Self, being empowered, being present, having gratitude, letting go of judgement and many other states of being feel like. Once you feel in tune with a thought, belief, emotion, feeling or any energy, you can choose at any moment to retune and stay in tune with that frequency. Sometimes we have to shed old belief systems and emotional baggage in order to allow ourselves to feel positive emotions and align to positive belief systems. Although, there is no need to wait. You can embrace these beautiful and freeing energies right now. You have the power to choose at this present moment what you are experiencing. You can ask your heart where you would like to be guided, and you can use your mind to move in that direction. Your heart can lead you, but your mind has to be in alignment and agreement with the heart in order to follow its lead.

Allow yourself to read this book at your own pace. Follow your own inner voice when you feel inspired to meditate, connect with your own heart, be creative, or practice forgiveness

Chapter One:
An Introduction of a Vision of Who We Are

Have you ever had this question in your mind *"WHO AM I?"* Many of the people who came to see me for sessions had that same curiosity which ignited my own curiosity to find "ME" as well. In retrospect, one of my clients travelled a long distance from Africa, taking 26 hours on a plane ride to the US in hopes of making the connection with his Higher Self by having a Quantum Healing Hypnosis session with me. He came in with only one question in his mind which was the most important question to him at that time. He asked Source, *"Who Am I?"*. What he received was heartwarming, which brought tears to his heart and his eyes. This event motivated me to find more of this same ultimate knowing, and that led to my own journey, which I will be sharing with you.

By the way, this man was in his early 50's, single, at the top of his career, but his heart was achy. He couldn't enjoy his success because people around him were suffering so much. His quest led him to find his truth by getting in touch with the Higher Self. It was truly my honor to serve him through QHHT.

He was satisfied and arranged for me to assist his brother afterward. I realized that his brother had very different life experiences than him, but his brother's heart was just as achy as his until the true self was discovered.

I will exclude the specifics of the story to maintain confidentiality, but it conveys my message perfectly. This encounter was the first spark of curiosity for me to start my own quest in searching for the same truth. I wished to have more expansive understanding (innerstanding) of resonance with the true meaning of life and its purpose. It was like the energetic chain of events in my circle had started because since then so many of my clients came in with that very same question in their list of questions that they wish to address to the Higher Self under hypnosis.

The Quantum Healing work that I do helps people make the connection with the Higher Self, the Divine Source, the Source of Knowledge while they are under hypnosis. In preparation prior to our sessions, I suggest my clients practice a daily meditation. I will explain in-depth the art and science behind the meditation practice in Chapter 3, The Higher Vision of Meditation, because it is one of the most important ingredients to help us reconnect and stay connected with the Higher Self. I also ask them to bring a list of questions that they would like to address with the Higher Self, including a request for self-healing. I use those questions to address the Higher Self during hypnosis to receive answers and assist with self-healing for them. I will also explain more about this in the next chapter about my journey with Source.

This quest has led me on a beautiful journey that helped me find my truth. The universe has been in partnership with me to help others find that same truth. I get to grow more from doing my work. This has turned out to be a soul fulfilling endeavor and became the ultimate reason why I do what I do, focusing on being of service to humanity. It is essential that I help people find clarity receiving the authentic answers from within. Nobody knows us better than the Higher Self, the Divine essence of us. It is both outside and within us. People connect with me, and then anchor the connection internally. I'm delighted to be able to help people to find their truth and give them the satisfaction of taking their life journey with hope, peace, harmony, joy and clarity.

I remember using a quote I heard once as a title for my essay in English class. The assignment was to visit an Art Studio on the campus and write an essay about the experience. My title was "*A Picture Says a Thousand Words.*" I admire the creativity of whoever came up with that quote. It inspired me to come up with one of my own, "*A warm heartfelt expression can be very inspiring and encouraging.*"

In the spirit of that saying I would like to share with you something precious that has raised my vibration and has been inspiring, encouraging and reminding me of why I must stay focused on being of service to mankind with the help of the universe. This was one of the updates I received from my client after our session.

She writes, "*May 11, 2019, Greetings Patti, I hope you are well and thriving and happy. I had a QHHT session with you in early February this year and I have been wanting to properly thank you. You are one of the most pure, radiant, genuine, and loving people I have ever met in this lifetime so far. I am so grateful for our session together as it has ignited my God-self embodiment. Thank you! You were so patient. You are truly a light in this world and being in your presence that day is something I will never forget. I wish you well. I am truly a different version of myself since that time - I recognize myself as God in form and a being of light. I know why I am here now. I have confidence in myself which is unshakeable because I don't doubt anymore. My gifts have turned on. And so much more! Thank you, Patti. I love you. Be blessed, dear one. In loving gratitude, (...signature...)*"

Every time I read this thank you note, I have deep gratitude that always brings joy to my heart and I often use it as a preparation or a conclusion during my talk with the client. I share this information to let my clients know that this reality can be theirs too after our sessions because of how the session is being conducted, and this is the same outcome that they can have if they allow it. I ask clients to be in flow with the process. I describe this process of how I utilize my gift of clairaudience to bring in the connection. It is simple, but extremely powerful. Since I am clairaudient, I am able to tap into the teaching from the benevolent Source that is truly loving and always there to help us with everything. We just have to simply ask. The love of Divine Source is unconditional and has a profound effect when we allow the connection to take place.

Her thank you card described my quote, **"A warm heartfelt expression can be very inspiring and encouraging."** This is one of the reasons why I wrote this book and created a YouTube channel on WHO AM I, because I utterly believe that the entire world needs to have this knowledge. We all need to remember who we are, why we are here on earth, and how we can leave this earth better than when we came in. I will always give a thousand percent of myself doing my work and I have given that same effort writing this book with my purest intention of helping all who seek the truth.

When I do this work, I utilize my gift of Clairaudience to receive the download from the

Source of knowledge/the Universe and I translate it into words to the people that I work with during our session. As I'm listening and engaging in our conversation, my client's spoken words project feelings that turn into vibration. The vibration turns into frequency. I have a natural ability to bring in guidance from the vibration of Source to help them understand themselves. Although, I bring in the same concept to everyone, the information in the downloads always translates at the level of frequency of the person I'm supporting. It is fascinating to hear myself talk about how many ways the same concept can be delivered and I love it. While I share messages with clients in a state of flow, I am also listening. I apply the new understanding in my daily life, and it is enchanting.

There have been many steppingstones that have delivered me to where I am now, giving me the confidence to do my work. One of those stones was the precious guidance brought forth by a medium during my session with him and his guides. This person is a famous psychic medium who channels his spirit guides. He utilizes his gift of clairaudience listening to his guides to help his clients during the readings. His guides have also helped him write many books to expand the reach of their teaching. After I read several inspirational books by this person, all transcribed from guidance he received from his guides, and watched the interview of him on

Discovery channel, I decided to have my own experience with his reading. How it works is that when he channels his guides during the reading, he repeats those words twice. This is when we know that the guides are giving guidance to us. I did not receive my guidance from his guides until the end of the hour. I could tell because he did not repeat sentences until the end of the session, but it was worth the wait.

The guidance I received from the guides was, *"He doesn't understand you, but we understand you and we will tell you what you need to know. You are intuitive. You hear frequency and interpret vibration. You translate it into feeling and vibrate it into images and language in the physical realm. You operate as an empath, as a vibration-ship to others that you work with. You serve as a conduit for the frequency."* I was intrigued to know what that means and wanted to be able to utilize it.

Months later I had a chance to talk to the Source of knowledge under my own hypnosis sessions. I will describe this experience in chapter 5, The Higher Vision of Patti's Connection with Source. I asked Source a question about my gift that perhaps I wasn't aware of. Source answered," *Patti you are Clairaudient*." And right away I replied back to Source like a little girl talking back to her parent, *"But I don't hear voices."* Source replied lovingly back to me, ***"But you hear frequency, don't you?"*** *"Yes,"* I replied. And Source said, ***"Own it! Claim it!"*** Right away I had an Aha moment understanding the meaning of my gift as I realized that this was the next stone that I was stepping onto from the statement that I received from the spirit guides earlier that year. At that moment I claimed it and I owned it.

Since then my gift has been more pronounced giving me a brand-new feeling. I've been doing my work with a greater confidence. I trust the universe. I trust the process and focus on being of service as a conduit serving others in the purest form of vibration-ship. I trust that the universe will always have everyone's best interests in mind and will give me the information to download with clarity in doing so. I realized that the spirit guides and Source guided me to my acknowledgement that I have this gift and I must use it to help people with it. So, if you are being entertained by my writing about my out of this world experiences, please take what you resonate with and let it inspire you to find your truth. Hopefully it will help you get to know your authentic self, so you can claim it and BE who you truly are.

I've helped more than a thousand clients at this point to attain self-awareness that led them to having self-acknowledgement. The majority of them become enlightened by the experience. It is very gratifying indeed to see wonderful changes in their beautiful souls. The change must be from within for it to last. I always remind my clients that the ball is in their court. This is not a band-aid. It is a permanent solution which requires change from the inner being to take place.

"We must be aware that thoughts become words, words become actions, actions become our character and we are what we believe[1]." This quote has been attributed to many spiritual masters and thought leaders including; Lao Tzu, Gautama Buddha, Ralph Waldo Emerson and Margaret Thatcher. It comes from the wisdom of the heart. I will repeat this often because it is necessary to keep reinforcing the change and keep it in motion. If things have not been working well in life, something has to be changed and the change must be made from its root and its root is the thought process. It has everything to do with perception.

It is obvious that if we still think the same thoughts, talk the same talk, act out the same actions, stay the same character and hold on to the same belief system, nothing will change. In order to make the change that

---

[1] Reference:
https://quoteinvestigator.com/2013/01/10/watch-your-thoughts/

creates a long-term effect, we must be aware that every situation has two perspectives, the perception of darkness or the perception of light. When we look at the situation from a perception of darkness, we will find an issue, a problem. If we have a habit of looking at situations focusing on the issue or problem, the darkness (the fear, worry and doubt) is magnified.

On the contrary, when we start looking at the same situation from the perception of light (the positive outlook and possibilities), we no longer see an issue or a problem, but only see the opportunity to grow. We are here on Earth to experience life. Everyone came into this world with the exact same gift from Divine Source to take on the journey with a gift of freewill! Nobody can make us think differently. Even Source will not interfere with what we choose to think.

Again, since thoughts become words, words become actions, actions become our character and we are what we believe, when we start making change by looking at things in the perspective of light, we will have an awareness of our own belief system. If our belief systems are not in alignment and do not serve us for the highest good, we can choose to utilize freewill to change that belief system. Our reality will change dramatically. We will have the new life experiences that are much more in alignment with what we want to manifest instead of incessantly manifesting what we don't want.

I will use the story of my own daughter as an example. I have not given her a QHHT session because she has not asked. I cannot help anyone unless they ask for help and want to be helped, because I can only help people to help themselves. I'm not the one who will be doing the work and making any changes. The ball is in their court. As a result, I can only teach my daughter by being the example and give her some guidance when she asks.

There was a time in her youth when she was still quarrelsome, she would say, *"Mom you are so annoying. There is a real world out there you know?"* I could only let her know that we share the world with others, but we do not have to share the reality. We can live in a different reality that we create and be okay with it. She was puzzled by that at the time. A few years passed. A friend she had known since high school was going through depression was in emotional crisis. It became so severe that her friend had an anxiety attack to the point that she could no longer work. The friend ended up locking herself in her home for weeks. Her friend called my daughter and asked her if I could help her with the anxiety attack that was ruining her life.

When my daughter asked me to help her friend, I did not hesitate to call to speak with the girl. I spoke with her for a couple of hours. Then later on that day, her mother brought her over to see me for the final help with hypnosis. The session was highly successful. Her friend went back home with a new perspective on life and was able to go back to work, traveling and living a joyful life. My daughter was puzzled with this outcome and she asked me genuinely, *"Mom, just talking to you for a few hours changed her life like that?"* I replied, '*YES*," but I didn't make any of the changes, she did! She was the one who made all the changes in her thought process and the belief about herself. I only helped her by showing and guiding her through it.

After that my daughter wanted everyone to come to talk with me. I had to explain to my daughter that I can only help people who want to be helped and are ready to be helped and ask for help. Again, this is because, I'm not the one who will be doing the work. She replied, *"But you can help anybody right?"* *"Of course,"* I said, *"but only if they are willing to make changes."* This is the incident that opened my daughter up to listen more and talk back less. She kept asking me to offer my help to the people that she knew when she read about their situations from her Facebook page. I had to remind her that I cannot impose my help on others because it won't work, and she finally got it.

Time has passed... a year or two later she called me on the phone frantically and asked me to talk to her husband, demanding that he must come to talk with me to get help. I calmly replied to her that he needed to ask for help himself and ask me to talk with him about it. I can't just impose my help on him. Then, my daughter handed her husband the phone and said to him, *"Mom said you have to ask for help if you want to be helped."* She handed him the phone and he sadly said to me, *"Ms. Patti, could you please help me? Could I come over to see you to talk to you today?"* *"Of course, sweetie!"* I said and I arranged to see him at the end of the day. I told him that I love him and would love to be a help to him.

He came over at the end of the day. He sat down, spun his fingers nervously and said, *"I never tell anyone about my personal problems, but I need help. I'm going to try to tell you my story the best I can. It is not going to be easy, but I will try."* I listened to his story attentively, compassionately and thanked him for trusting me with his secret. By the way, I was honored that my son-in-law would give me his trust and was very proud of him that he was ready to make some major changes in his life so he could move forward and thrive.

Later on, during our talk, I engaged into our conversation. I helped him hear his thought process of what was being said to support him in acknowledging the meaning of his spoken words. Again, because thoughts become words, words become actions, actions become our character and we are what believe. I showed him the two perspective within the darkness and within the light. I helped him understand that he has freewill. He can choose to look at things that have been happening to him in his life from a perspective of light. I showed him from that perspective how he could learn and grow from it. I let him know that we all get to learn and grow from our life experiences. Every mistake we make is our opportunity for a new lesson learned. If we do not learn from it, we will make the same mistake and it will become a pattern. These patterns become prisons if we do not change them.

I also showed him what he needed to see in himself and let him know my perspective within the light. I let him know that it is okay to make mistakes, learn and grow. I helped him raise his awareness and start a new way of operating by looking at things from the perspective of light and practicing forgiveness. I helped him understand that we can forgive ourselves for making mistakes and allow ourselves to make the necessary changes and grow in life, we set ourselves free from carrying the emotional baggage that will drags us down and prevents us from living a joyful life.

Also, when we forgive others who have done harm to us, we are not doing it as much

14

for them as we are doing it for ourselves. We get to set ourselves free from the hurt, the pain and the grudges from our emotional baggage. This way we will free ourselves and won't carry the baggage into other relationships we have in life with loved ones, family, siblings, co-workers, friends and others. My son-in-law and I finished our conversation within 90 minutes and at the end of our talk, he was smiling and said, "Wow! Ms. Patti, this is so simple! I've not been taught to see things from this perspective. Thank you so much."

Since then he has been committed to his new outlook in life, forgiving himself and others, thriving through his relationship with the people he loves. He worked on making changes and stopped the dysfunctional behaviors that caused himself and my daughter hurt and pain. He became pleasant and it showed. He was thriving through life with his new perspective. My daughter was in awe and kept saying to me that he is not the same person. This is so weird. He is a changed man! *"Mom, is this real? OMG!"* I asked her if it is a good way for him to be and she said, *"Yes, but it is so weird mom."*

A few months later, she called me asking for a different kind of help. She said, *"Mom, he has changed so much but I have not. I messed up. I kept provoking him by bringing up the past and I tried to make him feel guilty and kept blaming him for his behavior in the past.*

He is so angry at me right now." I had to remind her that this is a learning lesson for her as well. Since he has changed and become a new person, she must make some changes as well. She needed to let go of the past and stop bringing up the past and allowing it to interfere with the present moment. She needed to enjoy her husband with his new way of being and appreciate all the new wonderful experiences that she gets to have with him now. Do not dwell in the past that no longer has value. If she keeps giving power to the past by bringing it back, it will have the power to interfere and ruin her new life with him. She said, *"I know mom. I need to change along with it, otherwise I might bring the old person back in him and I'm not going to like that."*

A few months passed and she called me up again saying the same things to me. She was sobbing and described how she believes she really messed it up big this time. Again, still saying that he has changed so much, and she has not. She still brings up the past and it causes them a lot of misery. I let her know that she knows what she needs to do, and she needed to be committed to it. I told her that I love her so much that I would die for her. I will take a bullet for her in any moment, but I cannot make any of the changes for her. She is the only person that can make those changes and put them into action. She cried and said, *"I know mom. I know. I have to change myself to meet him where he is in order to make this relationship work."* Well, she must have done so. It has been more than two years and the couple just kept blossoming and thriving together. This is my family's personal experience that I feel the need to share with everyone. It is so precious to witness how simple life can be if we allow it to be. It truly is gratifying to see this change within my own family.

I would like to add that when my kids needed my help solving their problems, I never gave them a hard time about the mistakes that they have made but instead I always gave them the same support with unconditional love. Instead of solving problems for them, I helped them bring awareness by asking them this, *"What have you learned from it? Because if you don't learn, you will keep making the same mistake and it will become a pattern."*

Then we talk about the lesson learned and look into the possibility of what needs to be changed and be committed to that change. They will come up with their own solutions. I just have to remind them to commit to those actions. It is all about learning to have that awareness of one's thought process. This way we can develop an ability of cultivating wisdom. It is a lasting gift that can affect us in the long run, and it is a gift that keeps on giving.

It is from my purest intention to introduce this kind of information that will supports my writing about who we are. I would like to take this opportunity to be of service to all who seek for the truth so each can get to know One-self and thrive through life with simple abundance. As we remember and reclaim the Divinity in ourselves, we will be able to be of service to one another in light and in love, sharing joy from the loving heart.

The next chapter I would like to talk about my journey with Divine Source, the ultimate, the infinite, the purest and most loving energy and the purest. This has been the most meaningful journey on my path so far and I am very grateful for the experience which has helped me to know who I am. Ever since I claimed it, life has been absolutely precious. Most importantly, I get to help so many people with attaining the same insight to thrive and evolve through it as well. In the following chapter, I would like to offer readers the stories of my life experiences from the lows and the highs, which I believe many of you will resonate with.

I wish to deliver it using myself as an example of how I was able to turn my life around and deliver to the readers the tools that have helped me evolve through it. The low part in my story will demonstrate the darkness in my life, which I believe many of you can relate to. I would like to share with you how I overcame the darkness and turned it into a bright light. The high part of my story will demonstrate the light I have found. I believe many of you can resonate with it and perhaps are searching for a better understanding of how to get support from someone.

Everything I write about in this book is my truth. This truth has set me free from any blockages, and I was the one who was the builder of those blocks. I realized I was the one who got in my own way and turned myself away from the shining light. Please take the time to contemplate any part of my story and focus inward within yourself to see what you can do to make some essential changes in your belief system that will support you and set you free.

Chapter Two:
Patti's Journey with
The Higher Vision

Life is full of mystery - mysteries that are worth making a quest for answers to. My first big life mystery quest started when I was in my mid 30's. I had a life-threatening illness that almost ended my life's journey. I had a stress related health issue called Epstein Barr Virus triggered an autoimmune disease which shut down my liver. The doctor told me that I was literally stressing myself to death. It didn't happen overnight. It had been compounding over time with the combination of a toxic environment and self-sabotaging. It was suggested that I take bed rest and wait for a liver transplant. I was aware of the severity of my illness, but I had a 7-month-old baby, a pre-teen, a teenager and a hair salon business to care for. Not surviving was not an option; I needed to do something about it. I didn't want to stay in bed and most importantly, I didn't want to have a liver transplant. I decided not to give up on living just yet. So, I started my quest for permanent and long-term solutions which I could implement to help myself.

My condition was critical. I realized stress was affecting my well-being and I might die from it. I must find a way to combat it because my baby girl was only 7 months old and no one could raise her the way I planned to raise her with the love and affection that I never received from my parents. Because of my upbringing, and the way I looked at it from the perspective of darkness, I was living life from a negative belief system in a victim mode which contributed to my lack of self-love, self-esteem and self-confidence at the time, but I wasn't aware of it. I was carrying a huge load of emotional baggage. It was pretty bad, so bad that my subconscious produced nightmares trying to warn me about it.

I kept having the same nightmares over and over again that I was being chased by the thing. I call it the thing because I never got to see what it was or who it was. It was something that was chasing me, and I felt like it wanted to take my life. It was so scary, and I did not want to be caught. I would run for my life in every dream that I had. I would jump into a river to escape and when I floated up to the surface, it was still there waiting for me. Sometimes, I would run to the top of a mountain until I couldn't get any higher and when it caught up to me, I would make myself fly. Anything I could do to escape from the thing I would do.

In one of the nightmares I had, as I was lifting myself to fly from the top of the high mountain, I looked down and I saw lots of people doing their own things, living their own lives. It felt like nobody noticed me at all or if they did, nobody seemed to care about me. It was a very lonely feeling indeed. I kept experiencing the same nightmares with the same feeling that no one cared if I lived or died and I just kept trying to survive. There came a time when I had no other way to escape. I would wake myself up because I refused to surrender. When I woke up, my heart was pounding. I was sweating and shaking uncontrollably but relieved that it didn't get me.

The nightmare had gotten so bad and so extreme that I kept having to wake myself up in the middle of my dreams in order to escape from it and I would turn my pillow around hoping to not have to go back to those nightmares again, but it didn't work. It still carried on because my collective consciousness really meant business bringing it to my awareness. Can you guess who or what I was running away from? Well, I realized later on that I was running away from myself! I was afraid of my own shadow! My shadow that had been carrying a lot of baggage from feeling love deprived, feeling being let down, all kinds of emotional baggage. I don't even remember what it was anymore, because since then I've been able to let it all go. My shadow is no longer a scary one. My shadow is a happy loving shadow now that I've committed to doing the necessary self-work, learn to love myself.

All those years of feeling love deprived, I felt the need to have other people's approval which led me to have a lack of self-confidence, a lack of self-esteem. All that negative emotion became major emotional baggage that was highly toxic to my liver. As we all know our livers filter toxins from the body's systems for us. My system became overloaded with toxins. I was the one who created the toxins within myself. My poor liver couldn't filter anymore toxins for me. It completely shut down on me. My liver was not functioning. Instead my liver started to release the toxins back into my body.

My stomach was filled with the toxins, severely alarming my doctor. With his help and my cooperation, I learned to deal with stress better. We were able to release and drain out the toxicity that was blowing up in me. I found out later that if we had not been successful releasing the toxin, I would not be alive. To make the situation worse, my gallbladder took a toll as well. I had a major gallstone problem, and nothing could be done since I was not in any shape to receive surgery to remove it. I had to ride it out and see what would happen next.

I decided to start meditating during my hospital stay. Back then, I used to meditate every now and then just to help me manage stress. I did it when I felt like it or only when I had the time to do it. I only meditated when I thought I needed it, which wasn't enough. I just practiced deep breathing, focusing on the breath. I focused on turning my awareness inward to follow the breath, as I was breathing in and out, relaxing my body and mind. Every deep breath I took brought more oxygen into the body and every long breath I released took carbon dioxide and stress out from the body. More oxygen in the body helps improve T-cells and immune function. Less carbon dioxide is helpful in decreasing nervousness and may reduce the degrees of sadness that leads to depression and much more. Practicing deep breathing alone can balance the lungs and brain function, just to name a few benefits.

Moments after I heard the news from the doctor about stress being the main cause of my liver issue, in my hospital bed, I decided to be productive by practicing meditation instead of just lying around in bed having unwanted thoughts. It was a good thing that I remembered to do that, because before I started to meditate my blood tests showed an elevation of liver enzymes and the bilirubin level was going up, way, way up every day. That was extremely alarming to the medical team who understood its severity. After I started to meditate more and more in my hospital bed, everything just started to stabilize. Right then, I realized that I may have found hope.

Fortunately, it worked. Meditation managed my stress level, lowered my blood pressure and magically stopped the abnormal elevation of my liver enzyme and bilirubin level. That was astounding to me. I decided to meditate as if my life depended on it (literally) and I noticed an amazing improvement in my condition. I was more at peace with myself and was able to focus on getting well. In order to get well I was ready to work on letting go of my baggage (my negative beliefs, feeling of being victimized, hurt, pain, resentment, trauma and fear). Through this process, as I was able to let it all go, I felt lighter and so free. Free from the hurt and pain that I held onto for so long. Through this process, I realized that nobody was doing it to me. I was harming myself by thinking the same negative thoughts which all contributed to being love deprived that led me to have a lack of self-worth.

I was giving my power to a life situation and kept playing the same negative thought process as a broken record in my mind as if every situation was still happening in every moment. I thank my illness for waking me up to my truth. The truth that led me to love myself. I realized that self-love is the ultimate because it is the most important love of all. Self-love heals the self and opens the door to the soul, Higher Self, the Divine Source. The truth about forgiveness set me free. The truth of claiming my own power within and overcoming all obstacles with hope strengthened my ability to thrive through it all. I've learned a major life lesson; I cherish the process that has expanded my awareness allowing me to gain the insight about the unconditional love that exists all around us. It is extremely loving, and I would like to pass on this knowledge to others.

Before I move on to talk about my journey, there is something about letting go that I would like to add at this time. It is extremely powerful for us to know and to put into practice. This is how I was able to stop myself from drowning in my emotional turmoil that was so very toxic to my system and which shut down my liver. It is all about choosing to focus on being in the **Power of The Now**!

Being in the present moment is very powerful. Meaning that at this present moment, there is no past and there is no future. In this moment, the past is no longer here, and the future is not happening yet. Anything that has happened one minute or a million minutes ago is not happening anymore in this present moment. So, there is no need to bring in a story that creates an emotion that turns into a feeling of hurt and pain to interfere with the present moment. Some of us may live in the past allowing the thought process to recreate the old situation all over again as if it is still happening in the moment.

If we still play that memory in our mind like a broken record (like I did), eventually it will cause dis-ease and turn into illness like it did to me. We do not need to bring in the past that is painful and keep recreating it as if it is still happening. Let go of the story, let go of the hurt and pain. Forgive every one that did harm to us. Give a gift to self by forgiving, although you do not have to forget. Just forgive to set yourself free and remember what happened, how it happened and choose not to let it happen again. Letting go is the key to stop playing the broken record.

The future is an unknown and the unknown creates fear. Fear is not even real. It is an illusion. It is a product of the mind. Fear is just a perception we create in the mind. Our mind is so powerful, if we project it to be real, we will create it and make it real in our reality. Do not bring the future into the present moment by worrying about the future or be afraid of the unknown, because it will interfere with the present moment. The word present means gift! Give the gift of being in the present moment to yourself with love, peace, joy and harmony so that every moment that you are focusing on will bring those elements into the future. This is what you want to create in your mind and manifest in your own reality.

Speaking of fear, I have a story to share with you. I was having lunch in a restaurant with my lovely daughter and there was a big tall man that came into the restaurant asking for the owner of the little black car parked in front of the restaurant. I told him it is mine. Then he frustratedly said that he just hit my car and that, *"Every time I try to do something good for myself, the devil is always one step ahead of me."* I felt bad that he was so angry at himself, so I offered him a hug. I felt like I had to reach so high to hug him because he was so big and tall. Then I asked him how did he feel? He replied, *"I don't know. My wife is still going to kill me!"* With more compassion, I offered another hug. This time he reached down to hug me, and I asked him again if he felt better. He was softening now and seemed confused as he said, *"I don't know."*

I sensed that he was mellowing down, so I suggested that we go out to see the damage on my car. So, we did. He talked up a storm telling me the story of his life while we were getting all the info needed to make an insurance claim. Again, he said, *"You see what I mean? Every time I try to do something good for myself, the devil is always one step ahead of me."* I replied, *"Mister, there is no devil. It is only the negative thoughts in your mind."* He paused and looked at me with big eyes and said, *"Oh, I know. I preach that. I am a pastor, but I'm still afraid that that thing whatever it is will always be one step ahead of me."* So, I replied, *"Mister, fear is not even real. It is an illusion. It is the product of the mind, and you are so powerful. If you create it to be real, it will be as real as you create it to be."* He looked at me with a funny face and said, *"I preach that too."* So, I smiled and reminded him to just practice what he preaches, and all is well. After that he asked if I would give him and his wife a session and I had to tell him that I was on a short vacation with my daughter. No can do!

I share this story with you through another fun experience I had, to convey the message that we need to practice what we preach. We must walk the talk and maintain it. I find it easier to convey a message through example. Again, my intention to share each story from my very own experience is like painting on a canvas. Each painting will engage you to use your own creativity to resonate with the message being conveyed to you. Each one of you may perceive it differently and that serves the purpose because each one of us will have a story or two similar to mine and need to see it from a different paradigm and shift it into a particular perspective to see it and understand it better. It is all good. The bottom line is that it may serve as a conduit which brings out an emotion that the readers can relate to and be able to identify it within the self as a mirror image that reflects and highlights it and brings light to it (highlight = high vibration in alignment with light).

Moving back to my journey, being encouraged by my progress, and using meditation helped me tremendously to let go of the past. When I realized how helpful meditation was, I knew right then there must be many other ways I could help myself, and I was determined to find them. Fortunately, I found my next source of help. I was still very fatigued, but I was determined to see one or two clients a day to keep myself interacting with the outside world. Within one week of going back to engage with others, I saw a reserved and mostly quiet client, someone from whom I least expected to discover my next path. He told me that his wife was currently under the care of Dr. Yi Ping Hu, an amazing alternative doctor. His wife has been ill with the same illness.

For the last few years, they had been searching for help in both conventional and alternative medicine. By the time they found Dr. Hu, his wife's condition had already become chronic. Dr. Hu was giving her acupuncture and a freshly made herbal tea prescription that was custom brewed for her. Before he left the salon, he tapped his hand on my shoulder and said, *"Make sure you go see my wife's doctor as soon as you can. I will have my wife call you when I get home."* His wife called me to share her story. She sounded like she was crying while she told me about her condition, which she said she wouldn't wish on her worst enemy. She told me how to contact Dr. Hu and strongly suggested that I see her and start my treatments as soon as I could before my fatigue became chronic. Fortunately, Dr. Hu was able to work me in right away and I am forever grateful for the help I received.

Dr. Hu is a medical doctor from Beijing. She practiced both western and alternative medicine at Beijing Hospital in China. She has been practicing in the U.S as an acupuncturist and herbalist, and later on she wanted to give back to the community by teaching acupuncture for Maryland Acupuncture School in Bethesda, Maryland. From our first visit, I had a strong feeling that I would survive this illness. I intuitively felt strongly that she could help me handle this illness, which turned out to be true. She mentioned to me a year later that she used my case as a case study for her acupuncture students. My case demonstrated to them that miracles do exist, and I was her miracle patient. She and my traditional doctor didn't think I had a chance to survive this illness. Not only did I miraculously survive it, but I ended up not needing a liver transplant either.

While I was under her care, seeing her weekly for a whole year, I also took her Qigong classes that she was offering to her patients. I asked her, "*Why do you feel the need to offer these classes every Sunday on top of teaching acupuncture school on Wednesday nights on top of helping your patients in your clinic and when do you find time to rest?*" She replied, "*I don't have time to rest. In China, learning Qigong is a part of the medical curriculum. We must learn this self-healing method in order to enhance the ability to help patients. There is only one of me, but thousands of patients who need help. I feel the need to teach them Qigong so they can learn how to help themselves along the way. Also, I teach school on Wednesdays, because it is my way of giving back to the community. I want to make sure that some of the future practitioners learn it the correct way.*"

In conjunction with acupuncture and herbs, Dr. Hu's Qigong classes enhanced my ability to heal myself for a speedy recovery. At our first Qigong class, she asked us to put our hands together and measured them to see if all the fingers were equal in length. Then we held one of our arms up (I chose my left arm since I am left-handed) and started visualizing our fingers stretching far out into the universe, as she instructed. Later she asked us to put our hands together and measured them once again. My fingers were obviously not equal in length anymore; and the length has not been the same ever since. Fingers on my left hand are now about a quarter of an inch longer than the fingers on my right hand.

Right then I knew that Qigong was going to be my next new endeavor. I wanted to learn more about it. I studied Qigong diligently under her instructions and fortunately we had a Qigong Master from China visiting someone in the US and stopping by our area. Dr. Hu invited Master Wong to stay for a short while longer so that the master could teach her advanced students some of her advanced Qigong practices. Some of her students including me were invited to learn advanced Qigong from the great Master. The master had a short visit in town, so we were able to take only a few classes, but those few classes made a huge difference in my ability to practice Qigong and gave me one more tool to enhance and utilize in self-healing.

One of my most memorable encounters from this class was one day after we did the gathering Qi exercise (pronounced "Chi," meaning "Life Force"). She started doing her Qigong dance around us while we were standing a distance from each other with our eyes closed. As I was standing, receiving her Qi, I felt strong energy movements around me, and my body started moving around in a circular motion from my waist down. It moved faster and faster uncontrollably. We were informed later that she was enhancing our abilities to receive and hold on to the Qi with much less effort. We became a part of the Universal energy which is available to all life forces if we wish to receive, attain and utilize it to enhance our wellness and beyond.

I received one more amazing gift from the master. It was in another class when we were practicing receiving Qi in front of a building at sunset. We were told to look at the sun with our third eye and keep our physical eyes shut. Then the master started to do her Qigong movements. I don't know what she did, because my eyes were closed the whole time. By the time we were instructed to open our eyes and look at the sun, I realized that the sun I was seeing was dramatically different from the strong sun that we saw earlier. There was a beautiful soft white energy inside the sun and its energy was spinning out in a spectrum of colors, one color at a time in rotation.

The purpose of that exercise was to protect our eyes from any glaring light while driving at night so the light from other cars will not bother our eyes. I received a bonus package in that I am able to have the same experience and see the same thing all over again and again when I gaze at the sun. We can do this in the early morning and late evening to enhance our spiritual awakening. It is called "Sun Gazing". I Sun Gaze occasionally and every time it is spectacular as can be. The softness of the energy of the sun and the color spectrum around it spreading vastly into the beautiful sky was breathtaking, but in the meantime, powerful. It enhances my connection with the cosmos with the energy of the Qi that the Qigong method has to offer.

I have had a few opportunities to experience first-hand Qigong's miraculous healing. Most of my close friends are much older than I am, and one of them called me asking for my help because she was suffering severe symptoms from Shingles. This person was the one that introduced Dharmakaya Vipassana Meditation to me, which I will talk about in more detail later. She didn't know what I could do to help her, although she had faith that I could help her. Shingles is a reoccurrence of the chicken pox virus supposedly in people over 50. It is a condition involving an outbreak of a rash of blisters on the skin and it can be very painful.

I rushed over to see her at her home and offered to try to help her with my newly learned healing modality with Qigong energy. I was guided to bring her outside her home, and I started gathering Qi energy from the South (the way I learned it from class) and then placing the Qi on her body moving upwards and downwards without physically touching her as she was standing. I left her home right after I finished and didn't know if it would work or not. She called me 7 hours later to let me know that after I left, she went back to rest in bed, was running a fever and the pain was quite severe. It felt like small volcano eruptions bursting all over her body. She fell asleep and when she woke up the blisters were all dried up. I was in awe of her remarkable healing and I was so happy that it worked.

A week later, I had another encounter. My husband came home with excruciating back pain and said he didn't know how he was able to drive home in that condition. He looked very pale from enduring his back pain. I offered to try another Qigong technique and he accepted. After asking him to lie down on the bed with his face down, I started gathering Qi and then placed my hands on his back, visualizing heated energy going into it. I asked him what it felt like and he said he felt a warm sensation moving into his back. After I finished with the Qigong healing energy, I told him to rest and stay in bed for a while. I promised to check on his condition later. A half an hour later, he walked into to the kitchen and started doing something at the sink. I told him that he should be in bed resting and he told me that he was fine; the back pain had already subsided.

Again, one week later, a friend of mine who came for a visit had severe back pain. Her doctor had suggested back surgery. I offered to try to help her with the Qigong healing energy I had been having success with. She didn't think twice and was completely open to the idea. I was guided to have her sit on a chair with her back toward me. After I gathered the Qi, I placed my hands close to her back and started visualizing cold energy going into it. When I was done, I asked how she felt. She said that it was as if a chill was going into her back and right away her back pain subsided. I found out later that she did not need the back surgery. The pain was magically gone. I was in awe one more time of the mysteries of our universe, about which I was intrigued to learn more.

On my quests to innerstand (deeply understand something with heart and mind) the mysteries of the universe I came across another method that later on led me to QHHT and perhaps prepared me to be a dedicated QHHT practitioner as I am now. I studied Silva Mind and Body Connection founded by

Mr. Jose Silva. This made me much more aware of what our minds can do. It gave me a connection with the extra sensory that intrigued me more and more. From Mr. Silva's training, I learned to tap into my right brain, (the subconscious); that was my first encounter with self-hypnosis. I learned how to work with energy; increasing my ability in the areas of self-healing, remote healing for others, seeing an aura and most important of all, meditating more deeply and effectively.

In one of the Silva method exercises, we learned how to use our minds to levitate an arm without physically trying to move it until it reached the forehead. As I was using my mind to move my left arm, I started seeing a golden sparkling energy around it. As I was puzzled by it, I asked out loud to anyone who may have the answer to it. My fellow students and the instructor seemed to know about it, and all kept saying, *"You are seeing your aura. Are you seeing your aura?"* I had not heard of the word aura at that time because I was a newbie on this journey, so I asked again, *"Aura? How do you spell it?"* Again, they all jumped in to help me understand. Nancy, our instructor asked me about the color of the aura. It was yellow. She again asked what shade of yellow it was because each shade has a different meaning. I told her sparkling gold and she replied that identifies the color of wisdom. I was so excited about it and of course I wanted to learn more about auras afterwards. I have a story or two about auras to share here.

I realized that it was natural for me to see auras, but not at will. It shows up when it shows up because when I tried to see it, it didn't happen. One day, I was coming out of the bathroom, I saw my husband sitting alone on a sofa and there it was, a yellow-greenish aura around him. It wasn't a pretty shade. I would compare it to a color of infection in phlegm. I asked him about his mental status. He said he was feeling depressed at that moment. I guess he was supposed to experience, learn and understand it. I just acknowledged it, comforted him and moved on.

On another occasion, I was at a party at a family friend's home. I don't really like to party per se, but that was an important day for their family, and I wanted to be a part of it. A gathering was going on inside the home, I saw a spot under a willow tree in the side yard. I was drawn by the serenity to look at it and wanted to sit there to meditate. After I was done with my meditation under the tree, I opened my eyes and saw a beautiful pink energy expanding out from the leaves from all the branches and it felt lovely. It felt like the willow tree wanted to express the love back to me as it was receiving the wonderful energy vibrating from my meditation practice as my back was sitting against it. I acknowledged the feeling of love and gratitude that the tree had for my harmonious calm energy which I had projected into it. I still can see it in my eye's mind now like it just happened.

In due course, I was introduced to Dharmakaya Vipassana Meditation which I will refer as DVM (actually this is another synchronicity). The ultimate goal of this practice is to find enlightenment. This type of Vipassana Meditation is more advanced than the basic Vipassana practice I was already acquainted with. The late Luang Po Sodh, a highly respected Thai Abbot and a Buddhist monk in a very well-known temple in Thailand, was the founder of this method. He named it "Dharmakaya Vipassana Meditation," his method of teaching how to find the finest self within. "Dharma" has multiple meanings which you can look up from different sources, but I like this meaning best, *essential quality or character, as of the cosmos or one's own nature.* Also, I would like to give you my own definition the way I understand it.

"Dharma" is a part of the Buddha's teaching which I learned at a young age. It is one of the fundamental elements of which the world and is composed of the highest knowing. It is about mindfully practicing moral behavior. "Dharma" has been a part of my life which has given me guidance on living life with an awareness of thoughts and actions and also to practice moderation. Awareness is an essential quality and state to be in because when we are consciously aware of our thoughts, we are able to discern the things that are important to us; as thoughts become words, words become actions, and actions become our character and we are what we believe.

Practicing any methods of Vipassana Meditation enhances our ability to have self-awareness. This type of method, Dharmakaya Vipassana Meditation (DVM) practice has a unique meaning. "Kaya" in Thai means the body and "Dharmakaya" to me means the body of the one who has an awareness of highest knowing. When I became a part of this practice, I realized later on that it was to my blessing that I had an opportunity to tap into my Higher Self, the highest knowing. DVM prepared me to do the Quantum Healing Hypnosis work that I do now. DVM taught me how to be in alignment with the highest wisdom within me. QHHT carries the same concept. I learned how to help others to make the connection with the highest knowing, the Higher Self within them by opening an awareness to finding their own highest knowing (the truth).

Hypnosis is like meditation and every hypnosis is a self-hypnosis. It is about relaxing the body and mind deeply into a meditative level. During that time, we are lowering the brain wave to an Alpha level, the first altered state of consciousness which I will explain it in the next chapter on The Higher Vision of Meditation. This same information can be found on an episode of my radio talk show "Get It Straight from The Source" on Bold Brave Media (BBM) "Get It Straight from The Source". It is also posted on my YouTube Channel: Patti Intoranat. I named it "The Art and Science of Meditation[2]." In the video I share how it is essential to know how to support our spiritual growth through meditation practice as it will enhance our ability to reconnect and stay connected with our higher knowing or wisdom.

DVM is about focusing attention at the center of the body and combines three meditation techniques simultaneously. This leads to the goal of reaching higher and higher levels of concentration, enabling the meditator's insight to progress from a more worldly view to the highest level of innerstanding and ultimately to the highest level of wisdom. I would compare it to reaching Christ Consciousness (*know thyself*).

---

[2] Intoranat, P. (2018). *The Art and Science of Meditation*. Youtube Link
https://www.youtube.com/watch?v=KhzFUc_wLn8

This Vipassana Meditation Method was a Buddhist method. It was one of many advanced methods that I knew nothing about at the time. I had no idea that I would be learning something that could forever change my life and that later on I would also learn something with a similar concept to help others to make the connection with the Higher Self to assist in self-healing. I was able to completely self-heal my liver, and the gallstones magically disappeared.

I also want to give credit to Dr. Hu, who was helping me with her acupuncture, Qigong and Chinese herbs. I was receiving treatments from her on a weekly basis to help gain strength; taking her Qigong classes weekly to cultivate more energy, and also taking her freshly brewed herbal medicine tea daily to help dissolve the gall stones. I believe it must be a combination of everything that did the magic. I'm alive and well today because of all the help I received from everyone.

Normally, acupuncture and herbs are designed to bring back the inner balance of the body system, but that is a long-term goal. I was told that it may take at least a year to see the real solution. As fatigued as I was, knowing that gave me hope. Then shortly after I started learning DVM along with everything else, I began to advance more quickly. The recovery process took place within weeks. For this reason, Dr. Hu and my traditional GI doctor were surprised, and they called me a miracle patient.

I would like to take this opportunity to offer my heartfelt gratitude to everybody involved with my healing. I get to celebrate good health and having fun with my new journey with the help of wonderful people. I give thanks for having the life-threatening experiences as well, because that illness put me on this spiritual path; and now I am able to share my wisdom with others.

This type of meditation practice was my first turning point enabling me to experience Divine Source, although I did not realize it at that time. My intention was to find the way to combat stress and be healed from the illness. Instead I was able to make a complete turnaround of my life after I joined the DVM meditation group. That was the beginning of my precious new journey.

In retrospect, DVM practice came to me unexpectedly (another synchronicity of my endeavors!). A Thai couple stopped by at a yard sale at my former next-door neighbor's house. I heard the couple talking to each other in Thai, so I opened my window to say hello and later on invited them to come into my home for a chat, which I normally wouldn't do with strangers. One thing I asked them that day was whether they knew any places where I could study advanced meditation techniques that would help me with my long-term quest for learning about self-healing. They suggested a few places that I might look into. Later they graciously invited me to join their DVM group at their friend's home in DC, which was free to all of us. I remember saying to them that I would love to, but I don't know anyone in the group. They said, "*Well, you know us now.*" I jumped with joy and couldn't wait to participate (later on I was able to help the wife with her Shingles condition as shared earlier).

There were eleven like-minded participants that started the meditation group 2 years prior to my attendance. The meditation teacher, P' Somchai, was a deputy from Thailand to the US on a 4 years term. He was very well respected in the Thai community and deeply dedicated to the practice of this meditation. He started teaching DVM weekly at his home soon after he arrived in the US. Practicing this type of meditation came very naturally to me. The first time I attended, while I was sharing my experience with everyone during our post DVM practice, I noticed that all eyes were focusing on me. They asked, "*You did what? You could do that?*" I replied, "*Isn't that what we are all supposed to be doing?*" They replied, "*Yes, of course, but nobody gets that far.*"

They told me that they had been studying this method of meditation for two years and only one person could do what I was able to do, and it was not on her first attempt. Once again, I was in awe. I really think that the Silva Method had a lot to do with preparing me for it. Our kind-hearted meditation leader focused on my learning. He asked me to stay after each class and gave me instruction on the next step that I could work on at home. There are many steps that meditators must achieve in order to become more advanced, and they require a great deal of dedication and diligence. I had both! I was learning and practicing as if my life depended on it (and it did). I didn't want to have chronic fatigue and I had no desire to get a liver transplant (I was still receiving treatments from Dr. Hu). Well, to say the least, it paid off.

DVM was intriguing for me to learn and fun to practice. I learned to focus my mind at the center of my body and visualize aligning the mind with 18 different Buddha images. Later on, when I studied QHHT I learned that using the Buddha images deepened the suggestion Buddhists believe different ability levels and enlightenment occurs with the achievement of each level of consciousness. This is also my own revelation which I discovered years later while studying QHHT. Those bodies are my own higher consciousness which I now call my "Higher Self" (QHHT founder Dolores Cannon labeled this the Subconscious/Source of knowledge). In one of the lessons, I learned how to travel through time and space and to acknowledge my past lives, understanding and accepting the karma as my conscious mind stepped aside allowing my higher mind to take me places. This enabled me to innerstand what I needed to know to raise my consciousness, allowing me to merge with my Higher Self.

Consequently, my higher consciousness of mine showed me a past life that I needed to acknowledge that still has an important impact on my current life. Years later I gained a better understanding that this was very similar to a past life regression through self-hypnosis. I was able to accept all the issues I had from birth until that moment. I acknowledged the cause and effect and accepted the karmic debts I owed to everyone in my family and other people in my environment (a big group of karmic creditors, I suppose).

I accepted the outcomes as I was having the revelation and it helped me innerstand everything that I was going through in this lifetime. My biggest source of karma revealed through seeing my past lives was a past life as a Middle Eastern man who had a profession as an executioner. I executed people as ordered by a Sultan by cutting their heads off with a big curved sword. Many of those victims are reincarnated into this present lifetime with me to collect their karmic debts, because this is the life that we all get to work on our soul evolution the most and ending of karma.

It was in our soul contracts where we gave each other the opportunity to evolve at the soul level through utilizing our gift of freewill and making a different decision with pure intention. I'm happy to report that although it took years for that to happen, but it finally did. We are now free to live life with a much better relationship that I cherish. My birth family and I do not have many things in common, but we get to accept the differences within our values, and beliefs, and are able to co-exist without issues now. There are no more unexplainable hardships among us once all souls forgave one another.

Through my spiritual learning I know that now is a very special time on Earth when all souls have the same opportunity to release all karma by practicing forgiveness and ascend with Mother Earth to a higher consciousness in the New Earth. I will talk about the New Earth later on in the last chapter, "Higher Vision of The New Earth". The information about the New Earth will make sense after we have the understanding of all the matters prior to that chapter. It will be the ultimate reason for us to keep in mind as to why we are here co-existing on Earth, and offer the opportunity to teach and learn from one another so we can enhance and assist one another with the ascension process into the new paradigm called the New Earth of the Golden Age as some people describe it. There are many analogous concepts and words for these same ideas.

I had the opportunity to learn many other things from P' Somchai, a kind-hearted kindred spirit and Buddhist teacher. He taught me how to travel through time by aligning my conscious mind with the Higher Self (The Buddha images) so I could visit other dimensions. He taught me how to use mind power to help some of the troubled souls who are lost on the other side of the veil. I learned how to regress and progress my consciousness to a parallel universe to receive information for learning. I realized later on how much progress I had made in my spiritual growth. After a year of learning from P' Somchai, he told me that he had taught me everything he knew, and if I wanted to continue learning some more, I could contact his teacher, a Thai Buddhist monk, a meditation guru, who has expertise in highly advanced meditation practice who resides at a Thai temple in Long Island, New York.

Our group already had the opportunity to practice DVM with him, every once in a while, at P' Somchai's home in DC. P'Somchai did invite him to come to his residence to teach our group for an advance teaching and he also took us to visit his guru at the Thai temple in New York once. After P' Somchai finished his term and went back to Thailand, we invited the guru to come to my place to continue the teaching. This was the same time when I was having a fun time learning Qigong and made a new discovery that I am a healer. I excitedly told the guru that I had just learned that I could cultivate Qigong energy and direct it to help with healing for others and I want to help people with it. In return, he gave me a suggestion with great compassion, *"Why would you want to deal with other people's karmas when you still have your own to deal with? Overcome yours first!"* He was absolutely right and that was another eye opener to me, so I stopped and just stayed focused on my own spiritual quest for the time being.

Even though, I stopped going around offering help with Qigong energy I did not stop working on Qigong practice and harnessing the energy and I'm glad that I kept up with it. Qigong energy healing became very handy when my little girl was in the Children's Hospital in DC. She had a second episode of Kawasaki Disease. This happened when she was only 3 years of age. The first time she had this disease, she was only 1 years old. Kawasaki Disease is very rare, it is known to develop in mostly Asians or Asian-Americans and mostly in boys under 5 years and younger. It is even more rare for girls to have it and it is extremely rare for anyone to have it twice. The symptoms are similar to Streptococcus. The difference is that Streptococcus is a bacterial disease and it can be treated with antibiotics, but Kawasaki Disease is a viral disease, as a result, antibiotics do not work as a treatment.

She had the classic symptoms such as: strawberry tongue, rashes, high fever, swollen Lymph nodes, red throat, and loss of appetite. Her Pediatrician sent her to the ER because she had a high fever of 104.7 degrees. Unfortunately, she was diagnosed with the rare disease once more. She was treated successfully with hemoglobin intravenously the first time, although this second time her body rejected the treatment. It was critical for her to be able to receive hemoglobin intravenously, otherwise there was a possibility that she might die. I was there with her in every moment and even laid down on her hospital bed holding her in my arms. Her situation was getting worse and I realized that perhaps some kind of intervention was needed. I did what I knew best.

I combined every modality I knew at the time like a cocktail working with energy. I utilized my mind using both methods of bringing the Divine energy of Dharmakaya and harnessing Qigong energy at the highest level that I possibly could. I was serving as a conduit between those energies and my daughter. It worked! The only reasonable explanation that I can come up with is that the energy that went into my daughter helped raise her vibration which sparked her immune system and miraculously her body no longer rejected the treatment.

After a few hours of hemoglobin slowly dripping into my daughter's system intravenously, she started to show signs that she was getting better. I'm very grateful for that experience. It raised my belief and trust in the powerful of the mind and the healing energy of the universe, around us and within us. This energy is everywhere as Nikola Tesla stated. It is so pure that when we place a pure intention to tap into it and ask for help, its purity can do wonders. It is magical and I learned to believe it and trust it. This experience provided me with another steppingstone, building on my belief system and proved to me that there is definitely power in a mind with pure intention and that anything is possible.

Another phenomenal experience I had that wows me every time I talk about it was when one of my daughter's cats was dying. He was seriously ill with kidney failure. He was deteriorating rapidly over a few days starting with not eating, drinking, not using his litter box and later on my daughter found him unconscious face down in a litter box. He probably felt the need to use his litter box, but his elimination system did not work anymore so he just collapsed there from trying. She took him to the Veterinary hospital. Dr. Chris, the Veterinarian didn't think her cat, Masuka, would survive. The diagnosis was poison in the system. It could be from plants or something else that he ate, and yes, Masuka had a habit of chewing on plants. Dr. Chris said there was only a 1 percent chance for him to survive this illness and that 1 percent chance would only be from a miracle.

Dr. Chris was a truly compassionate doctor. He went in every few hours at 1 am, 3 am and 5 am to check on Masuka. Dr. Chris thought her cat would be dead by dawn. I went to visit his lifeless body at the hospital in the early morning and the only thing I could do was just lovingly talk to him. As I was talking to him while looking him in the eyes, his eyes became responsive, opened and shut a few times. I sensed an opportunity to have an energetic connection with him at that moment. Since, I was the one who gave him and his brother the most care when they were young, the strong bonding was already established like a grandma to the boys.

I started talking to Masuka with the purest intention to communicate with him at the soul level and it worked. Using the power of the mind to connect and communicate with him turned out to be a brilliant idea. I said to Masuka as his eyes were peering into mine, *"Sukie, you are very ill. Dr. Chris is giving his all. We are giving our all. We love you very much. I love you very much. We would love to have you with us longer, but I also respect your freewill. If you want to be with us longer, you need to give us your all. You need to pee it all out. You need to release the toxins in your body."* He winked at me and I decided to perform Pure Bio Energy healing on him before I left for work.

By the way, Pure Bio Energy is one of the healing methods I learned. One of my hypnosis clients introduced me to this healing modality, and of course, I had to try it. In this method, I learned to become a conduit for Source energy and harness the pure energy from Divine Source, bring it into the person's body (in this case it was our cat's body) and let Source energy take care of anything that needed help. Again, I was new at this, but I did not hesitate to give it a try, and it was proved to be helpful.

My daughter called me on the phone a little over an hour after I left the hospital explaining the situation excitedly. She described how she was holding him on her shoulder like she normally would do, and he urinated on her. She went home to get changed and came back to the hospital and he kept peeing on her. She said she never thought she would be this happy having a cat pee on her all day long. I went back to visit him that afternoon and he tried to get up to greet me, but he couldn't. He seemed to have some energy after Dr. Chris fed him through an IV and after he was able to release the toxins out of his body. In retrospect, I had to do the same thing, releasing the toxins out of my system when my liver shut down. My doctor was pleased when it happened. Otherwise the toxins would have accumulated and destroyed my entire system and killed me.

Our communication started taking place again at that moment. I said to Masuka, *"Thank you for choosing to stay around and thank you for giving your all and peeing it all out. You need energy."* He winked back at me, so I talked to him some more, *"You want some food?"* He looked at me and moved his mouth up and down making noises to respond. Btw, Masuka is a fat cat. He loves food. So, I asked him again, *"You want to chew some food?"* and he meowed back. I noticed a bowl of wet food inside his crate and I knew he liked dried food; that's why I asked him if he wanted to chew so I requested dried food and some water for him.

He almost finished his food and drink and continued to improve.

Dr. Chris said he then had a 50/50 chance to make it and the next day his condition improved to be a 60 percent chance. Then on the fifth day he was sent home. Dr. Chris asked us, *"What did grandma do? It was grandma! She did something."* I did not know what to say, but just smile and said, *"Grandma's LOVE healed him."*

This story is memorable to our entire family and we all called Masuka a miracle cat. Coincidently, I'm cat sitting this weekend for my daughter as the mold in her home is being cared for. I get to have the honor of keeping her cats for a few days, so the boys are here and Masuka is laying right on me as I'm trying to write his story. He probably wanted to make sure that grandma did not miss a thing. He is purring so loudly right now. I wish you could hear him. He is sharing his love to you all right now. See if you can feel his energy as you are reading. LOVE heals! Btw, I learned from one of my clients' Higher Self during hypnosis that, *"Cats are the type of animals that are energetically closest to Source."*

Later on, I came across another kind of energy healing modality. I was introduced to Reiki, which once again added to my incredible experiences with energy healing. Reiki is a life force energy; Reiki practitioners can be attuned to receive. The practitioners become a conduit for life force energy to help others with their healing. I came to understand that it is the same energy as Qigong. Qigong is a Chinese method, utilizing life force energy from the original life force energy of the frequency signal and Reiki is a Japanese method of utilizing the same energy force. I was already intrigued with the idea of bringing the healing energy from Source to help people and animals with healing, so I decided to go all the way and became a Reiki Master. I really enjoyed the learning and the practice of utilizing life force energy. It has continuously inspired me to want to know more about how the universe works.

As I was studying Reiki, an acquaintance introduced me to Dr. Brian Weiss' book, "Many Lives, Many Masters". The book is about the Past Life Regression that he conducted on one of his patients. Dr. Weiss is a Psychiatrist who accidentally stumbled upon a past life as he was trying to help his patient, Catherine, which resulted in him finding the unknown causes of her issues. He practiced traditional regression hypnosis at the time and wished to help her regress back to the time beyond her conscious memory of what happened, beyond what she could remember. He was hoping to regress her back to the earliest time since birth.

To their surprise, she regressed back into many lifetimes during the course of the year of treatment. Catherine was able to self-heal much of her emotional trauma during her regressions, experiencing multiple lifetimes that identified the unknown issue in her present life, caused by carrying the cellular memory forward into this life. He was dumbfounded by the new discovery and wrote this book in the late 1980's. It is still popular decades later. He wrote many more books as he kept progressing, and of course, I read every one of them. He became one of the forerunners to teach and take people through the exploration of Past Life Meditation and has been conducting national and international seminars and experiential workshop as well as training programs for professionals for years.

Dr. Weiss and his patient thought they were doing the regression of her present life. It came to both of them as a surprise that his patient regressed back to many lifetimes. I could relate to her story because of my own regressions through DVM practice. I knew right then that I must learn how to do it. It felt like this is the path I must walk. It gave me the confirmation that past life regression is a real deal, many can benefit by it and I want to help others with it the way I have helped myself.

I found a hypnosis school in my area and was able to complete the training and become an International Medical and Dental Hypnosis Association Certified Hypnotherapist (IMDHA CHt). I specialized in Past Life Regression. Even though I was able to regress people to see their past lives successfully, I didn't know how to make a connection to the self-healing that they needed as I had personally received it. I was determined to find the missing link, and voila, thanks to the technology age that we are in, I came across Dolores Cannon and her information captured me entirely. I believe it was in 2011 when she was launching her new book, "The Three Waves of Volunteers and the New Earth". My friends and I travelled to attend her lecture about her book in Front Royal, Virginia. Again, I was in awe, intrigued, inspired by the whole experience. I stood up to ask questions during the lecture and was excited to learn that there would be a QHHT level 1 training in a few months in the East Coast area.

I couldn't wait to sign up for her class. I just couldn't pass it up. I travelled from Maryland where I reside to attend her classes in Andover, Massachusetts. I had a strong sense right away that her method was perfect for me as it felt like second nature to be learning it. That same night after I had learned her technique, I had an opportunity to practice on a couple of my classmates. I assisted one of them in trying it out on me, since I was already comfortable with past life regression technique. I wanted to make sure that I would have a good experience with a successful regression. Consequently, we all had confirmation that her method worked magically. My classmates and I, all had successful sessions and were able to call in our Higher Selves and receive mind-blowing messages.

The phenomenal part of my own experience that time as I was under hypnosis was that, as my Higher Self was calling in, I started to feel weightless like I didn't have a body at all. It felt as if I was floating on my hotel bed where we were conducting the session. It was definitely an aha moment for me. I just loved it. It was very satisfying. I shared my wonderful experiences in front of the class the next day. I just felt "wow"! I had so much fun doing it. I shared my experience with the class of what it was like as I was a facilitator to the two classmates and also what it felt like being a hypnosis subject. Dolores kept asking me questions as I was telling my story, such as, *"Well, okay, what did you do? ...And how did you handle that? ... Okay...What did you do? ... You did a great job!"* Wow, after that I couldn't wait to come home to do more regressions.

In another session of mine, just recently, as the Higher Self was receding, I started to feel like weight was coming back in and at that time and before that, during hypnosis, I did not feel like I was being hypnotized at all. The experience I had at the end gave me a confirmation that I was. This particular experience helped me understand how some people may have doubts. I had to experience that to understand the feeling. I too was wondering how well that session of mine worked. If I hadn't felt my own energy shifting like that, I probably would have had doubts too. I believe everything happens for a reason and serves a purpose and this incident held a purpose for me. Its purpose was to help bring my awareness to some of the experiences that others might have, and it was for me to understand how doubt could arise in a hypnosis subject.

The advanced meditation practice of DVM was a steppingstone to my Quantum Healing Practice. It was the undeniable experience I had with DVM that helped me with my self-healing. I had a chance to have a first-hand experience of a past life regression under a deep meditation, but at that time I was not aware that such things like that could be done. I was taught to make the connection and became ONE with the Higher Self (in Buddha images at that time because the learning was purely in Buddhist teaching) and to observe my inner self.

In retrospect, it felt like I was in a hypnotic trance, but wasn't aware of it because I did not know anything about hypnosis at the time. I realized later on that Meditation and Hypnosis are so similar. We get to put ourselves in an altered state of consciousness. When we are able to relax our body and mind, our consciousness shifts into an altered state of Alpha level. I will explain more about Alpha level in the next chapter, "The Higher Vision of Meditation."

With the practice of learning how to be ONE with the higher self, I also learned to travel with my mind, tapping into the Source of Knowledge. A past life experience was shown to me during one of my DVM practices, which helped me with a realization that that particular past life I experienced was there for me so I could learn something very important about myself. I was able to observe and acknowledge it. As I accepted and came to terms with it, ultimately, I received a quantum healing from it. Miraculously, through that experience I had, my liver, somehow, instantaneously healed itself. Even my GI doctor couldn't understand how my liver was completely healed like that.

All of my new blood test results were back to normal and showed no sign of the illness that I was having not that long ago. He and other doctors called me their miracle patient for that reason (like Masuka). I could not and would not be able to explain to any of my doctors (who could only understand science medicine) of how I tapped into my mind to experience my other life in the past and was able to receive an instantaneous self-healing as a result.

How could I tell them that I experienced a past life regression during a deep meditation and learned a great deal from that? How could I tell them that a simple choice I made to forgive myself and others after acknowledging what happened in the past was the ultimate solution that I received for self-healing? How could I tell them that it happened because at that moment heartfelt forgiveness shifted my reality and raised my vibration to the new consciousness that led me to wellness? How could I tell them that forgiveness ended my karma? I couldn't, because I did not know anything about that either. All I knew was that all symptoms of my liver illness magically disappeared.

My phenomenal experience led me to a new journey that filled with amazing truth that I would not have had the interest to tap into if my survival did not rely on it. Not only did I survive it, I thrived through it. Since then, I've learned an important lesson about forgiveness. I also learned how to love myself. Self-love is the most important love of all. I learned that when we love ourselves, we will not self-sabotage. We must forgive ourselves for making any mistakes from any circumstances and allow ourselves to learn and grow from the experiences with love, instead of getting mad at ourselves from making a mistake big or small. I acknowledged what I did, and I must ask myself what I've learned from it and if I would do it again. Many times, the answers were "probably not", but sometimes I giggled to myself and thought "*Well, it was a fun experience. Perhaps, I may try it a few more times.*" Then, I accepted the lesson and moved on.

I'm now aware that LOVE heals everything. So many people lack this beautiful feeling of the LOVE of self and I was one of them, but not anymore! I now know how to love myself unconditionally and it is definitely over-flowing to others around me. I give that same love to others naturally. Now, I live a joyful, meaningful life, and it keeps getting better every day in every way. With my strongest desire and the purest intention, I wish to pay it forward to show you how.

I've learned that we all need to wake up to our truth. We need to find the power of the loving divinity within us more than ever right now. We need to inspire and share our knowledge with one another. From practicing the Quantum Healing Hypnosis Technique, I realized how similar QHHT is in comparison to DVM. The QHHT method puts people under a deep trance and engages their minds to take a soul journey. By regressing the soul back to a different lifetime, the most appropriate time and place will help them receive information that they can learn from. The information so potent that it leads to the self-healing like it did for me. The connection is made between their conscious mind and their subconscious mind to cause self-healing. I will explain more in depth about exactly how this works in the next chapters. I will need to engage you into an understanding of the multi levels of consciousness and the ultimate power of the divine sparks within us that are a part of us.

My DVM practice is similar to QHHT in that sense. As I took myself to a very deep level of consciousness; I was able to regress back and take a soul journey to witness my own previous lives that helped me understand the cause of my suffering in this life. It was the residue from my past lives that still had an effect in my present life. Through the understanding of my past lives, my conscious mind and subconscious mind made the bonding connection, therefore, I was able to gain the wisdom I needed to overcome the hardships in this lifetime. My healing was real, and I am alive and well to write about it in this book. My clients' experiences through our sessions are real to them too and many of them are able to thrive as a result of them. With those experiences, I became passionately dedicated to practice QHHT and wish to help people with it.

My journey in pursuit of the higher self really took off right after my training with Dolores's Quantum Healing Hypnosis Technique. Her technique is timeless, unique and powerful. I was blessed to have the opportunity to learn it directly from the great master, my late teacher, Dolores Cannon. She was a pioneer in this type of hypnosis work. She was also an author, teacher, international lecturer, UFO investigator, and her work kept evolving throughout those 50 + years of practice. She passed away in October 2014, but her legacy is still very much alive. Her work is well known all over the globe.

People have been touched by her work and more and more people are still intrigued and inspired by her message. Thanks to modern technology; we have the world wide web, YouTube channels, podcasts and other media. You can read her books or watch her YouTube videos released by her family. Just type in her name and you will find them. Her QHHT method reminded me of the advanced meditation practices I practiced which supported my own quantum healing for the serious illness that I had.

Dolores' QHHT technique helps people make the connection with the Higher Self to receive self-healing and receive answers to their questions. It felt natural for me to get into this work because I already had my own phenomenal experience from the practice of DVM. I didn't even know how the meditation that marvelously healed me actually worked until I learned the practice of Quantum Healing. Now I realize how DVM works, there is a modality to help others in a similar way (QHHT), and I have found them both.

When I came across her work, I was inspired and motivated to learn her technique so I could help others with it the way I helped heal myself. It was quite a blessing and an honor that Dolores and her team selected me to be one of the six people that she wanted to personally train, so she could launch her new pilot program. She called it "Recommended Dedicated Practitioners" at that time (now that program has a new name and it is called Level Three Practitioners).

What inspired Dolores to launch this program was that she had a sixteen-year waitlist and she was already in her 80's. Her clients told her that they could not wait 16 years to see her for help and wondered if she could recommend any of her practitioners that could effectively work her method like her. She told them that she couldn't because she didn't know how her students work and she added that each one of her students brings his or her own niche into this practice. She described how she taught them all the same, but she did not know how they work with what they were taught. That was when she realized that she must find the way to be able to recommend some people. She invited 6 of us to receive personal training from her. None of us were aware of her plan. All we knew was that she and her daughter, Julia, wanted to see us.

Since it was a pilot program, we were together sitting in a round table environment and she used our video sessions sent to her prior to our meeting as a teaching tool. It was her brilliant way to teach us the do's and the don'ts. She marked down by the minute as the video was playing to note what she wanted to show us. She asked us for input on what we saw and to test us as whether or not we saw what she saw. Some of the videos obviously showed what not to do and we all got to evaluate each video with her. She explained clearly what would happen if we made that mistake. She pointed out the actions of the subject (client) to help us understand what was going on and why it was happening that way.

Her evaluation was precise. She watched our videos attentively and marked down by the minutes as the story which was being played out during regression. To my surprise, she used my video to point out the actions during regression that were happening to the hypnosis subject as it was happening in real time. She showed us the natural reaction of the subject as the scene was intense and the feelings and the emotions were very real.

The learning environment was nurturing and comforting. I felt her love and pure intention the entire time. She was a woman of high integrity. She wanted us to know before we started that this would be a pilot program that she wanted to try out. It was absolutely heartwarming to experience her purity during this training. Not only had Dolores gifted us with the intensive training during those 3-day weekends, she also sponsored all of us with lodgings and meals. Her intention was to personally train us as her apprentices. She was devoted to being able to comfortably endorse us to her client. She had all the clients' best interests in mind, and it showed. She launched the program on January 1, of 2014 and passed away the same year on October 18. She left her legacy behind. I am dedicated to carry on her work with the same level of integrity and devotion.

In retrospect, I was quite nervous when I received her invitation to go to Arkansas to receive personal training from her. I felt like her bar was so high, and I questioned how I could represent her at her level, although I really wanted to. I was nervous about meeting up to her expectations. It made me feel like I had to find a way to prepare myself to keep up with the learning and to honor her work. Apparently, a surrogate session came to mind. It was still fresh to me because I had just recently learned that technique during the QHHT level 2 advanced training in Arkansas. There were 160 students in that class and one of her teachings was to hypnotize someone as a hypnosis surrogate subject for a client. She told us that she received this information from the Source of knowledge that we could do a surrogate session for others.

Let me bend your mind with the explanation of how it works. We would need to find a close friend or a family member of the client who is willing to volunteer to be a surrogate subject for the person. Then we would attempt to hypnotize that person as a surrogate subject to receive the answers and request the healing from the Source of knowledge for the client. (This is one of the examples showing us how she received her advanced information to teach us continuously. I feel so blessed that after her passing, I seem to be able to tap into that same knowledge that advanced my growth.) I have total trust in Source like Dolores did during her practice. I will elaborate more about this mind twisting advanced method in Chapter 5, The Higher Vision of Patti's Connection with Source.

On the other hand, I was wondering at one point if she has become One with the Source of knowledge on the other side of the veil and still actively teaching us through the connection of the subconscious mind. Sometimes, some of my clients who have Clairvoyance would tell me during our sessions that they could see her standing on my right side. On top of that, during one of our sessions, Source said, "*Dolores is working with us now.*" It did not surprise me at all to hear that.

The surrogate session technique is very advanced. Many have tried it out and did not have the same level of success. The purpose of Dolores teaching us to hypnotize a family member or a close friend of our client as a hypnosis subject is to be able to help someone who may not be able to go under hypnosis. The person whose conscious mind is too strong and won't give up control leads to not having the ability to let go and to relax which blocks self-hypnosis from taking place; or someone who is under the age of sixteen where Dolores said that they may not have the maturity to handle the experience and to understand the information that comes through, or someone who lives a long distance away and cannot be in present in person, but is urgently in need of help.

I had a few opportunities to try it out in multiple ways exactly the way I was taught and had some success that blew my mind, but not always, because some of them may not honor the information from their family member who became a surrogate subject for them and still believe that this is all made up by the mind. The skeptical mind can be good if it is done reasonably, but when the skeptic is not flexible and the mind is not open to anything, there is nothing anyone can do to change that unhealthy negative belief system. This happens when I work with someone who has a habit of doubting everything to start with, if the subject does not go deeply into the Theta level (a somnambulist level, the deepest level of trance that cannot recall anything that happened during hypnosis afterwards) the information received may be explained away and not honored by the person.

I am an inquisitive person just like Dolores and I like to try things out to satisfy my curiosity sometimes. I realized that with her technique, I could try it out on me. I arranged to have my friend, Sue, become my surrogate subject. My intention was to ask the Source of knowledge to prepare me to meet with Dolores for the advanced training (that I was feeling honored to have the opportunity to do). I did not know how well it was going to work, but I had nothing to lose. That surrogate session of mine turned out to be something that has forever changed my life and the lives of many others.

Sue, who was my surrogate subject, happened to be a true somnambulist. I would compare her with the late famous Edgar Cayce, the sleeping prophet (a nick name given by a biographer). Edgar Cayce induced himself under a deep state of hypnosis and was able to make a connection with what he called the mind of the soul to retrieve knowledge from the spiritual realm where all subconscious minds are connected.

She went into the Theta level so deeply that she could not recall anything afterwards. Luckily, I used my phone to video record our entire session that lasted for two hours. I used it for my material requested by Dolores and sent it in to her to be evaluated for our special training. As I was playing around with my new endeavor, I realized that I tapped into the Source of knowledge and worked with the Oneness of Source consciousness. Meaning that all become one at that level of consciousness, Source, Sue, and myself where we were enabled to tap into the Akashic record of the person who I requested the help for. In this case it was for me.

The Akashic record is like an enormous photographic film of all experiences of our planet and the people in it. It can be personalized to the unique record of one person and it has the record of the person in every moment and in every lifetime that the person has lived. I realized after our training as Dolores suggested that there was a lot of information we could dig deeper into, although I was not aware of the opportunity at the time, but I was very proud that she used my video as a teaching tool to show the six of us during the round table discussion.

She marked down the minutes of the highlight that she wanted to show us in the video. She pointed out what was happening and why it was happening. She explained how my surrogate subject became that character in the scene and how Sue's body reacted naturally as everything was happening in action. My purpose of doing a surrogate on myself was to prepare me for this training and I realized afterwards that what I'd received was beyond my wildest expectations. Dolores asked me why I did it this way, because I was not taught to do a self-surrogate. I giggled and told her that it was because I could, and because I was so nervous that I needed to see if I could prepare myself for the training. She acknowledged me quietly and moved on.

We had an amazing training and felt so loved and cared for. Dolores and her daughter, Julia, left their footprints in our hearts and I'm forever grateful for the beautiful gift they bestowed upon us. The learning experience, the skill, the ability to help people to reconnect with the Higher Self to self-heal and we get to pay this gift forward to so many people.

We had to come back home to do more work and improve on the areas she pointed out to us. Then we had to send a new video session back to her to prove that we met up to her high standard in order to receive her approval. I was in awe to receive her positive feedback to every area, but I wasn't sure if I passed because she did not say anything about passing in the email. I checked with my other fellow practitioners about her feedback in my email. Did I make it? Did I pass? Did she approve it?

My colleagues replied back to me that they think I made it because the rest of them received the feedback of how they did, but they were told to refine their skills in particular areas and needed to send the videos back to her again to be reevaluated. I realized then that I made it. I really made it! The next step was for me to wait until the rest of our group completed the work before she would launch her new pilot program, "Recommended Dedicated Practitioner". I am very honored to represent Dolores, to be one of her proteges, and able to utilize her precious skills in helping others with her method. I will carry her work and keep her legacy alive with the same integrity and intention that she had to always have the client's best interests in mind.

After my experience with having Sue as my own surrogate, I have to admit that I became dedicated to conducting my own sessions through a surrogate. Sue and I have been getting together every couple of months and each time I cherish it as much as my first time. Each experience is an enlightened experience. I enjoy learning more about myself and the more I learn about me, the more confidence I have. I am fully aware of why I am here and what I have to do.

On top of that, it helped me so much with my personal growth. I kept working on my progress to grow spiritually. I remember the time before I was ill over 25 years ago, on a scale of one to ten, ten being the highest, my self-love, self-confidence, self-esteem, self-acknowledgement, self-awareness were minus something and now after the work that I've been doing with the help of the Source of knowledge, on that same scale I am at the level of infinity because ten has limitations for me now.

I have not had a bad day for so long. Even though, there have been plenty of potential for days to be bad. Since I have practiced raising my awareness, I've learned to accept other people's belief systems, without judging them. It has helped me stay grounded from within and be true to myself. The ability to discern the content of the duality has helped me acknowledge which one I want to walk away from and which one I choose to be a part of, has brought me a profound peace and harmony. The ability to stay on the observation deck to observe people's behaviors and intentions and not allow myself to be entangled with some people that I'm not in alignment with is priceless. I have been able to stay grounded from within.

As I've been working on that growth for myself and have claimed my divine light, my life keeps getting simpler. Simplicity brings joy! I definitely have become more balanced and centered and of course I have more JOY in life. Joy is a simple abundance that is always available. Of course, it is our Divine right. You just have to be energetically aligned with your Divine Source, and I will show you how it works throughout this book.

Through this journey of mine, I've learned to be in flow with the universe. I described my gift of being clairaudient earlier that I hear frequency and interpret vibration. I translate it into feeling and vibrate it into image and language in the physical realm. I operate as an empath, as a vibration-ship to others that I work with. I serve as a conduit for the frequency. I get to hear myself talk as the translation comes in. I value it and I apply it in my own life. The result I have seen and being recognized by others has led me to live a meaningful life. I focus on being of service to others and maintaining my light.

When I say I have not had a bad day for so long, it is because I do not let things bother me the same way. I learn to look at every situation within the perspective of light and staying in my present moment in joy. This is the same practice that I would like to pay forward to anyone who seeks it. Many of my clients become enlightened by the result of getting to know more of the powerful loving self and utilize their freewill to choose those options.

Enlighten means having great knowledge, innerstanding. When people have an in-depth innerstanding of self, they will be more at peace and harmony. They will be able to make better decisions in life based on love instead of fear; compassion instead of anger and harmony instead of disharmony. The results will be much more in alignment based on their true feelings. When the self-acknowledgment and self-awareness are there and knowing that we have freewill to choose how to react or not react to things and be able to look at everything from the perception of light, life will be amazing.

I'm devoted to helping others to find this authentic truth within them and help them through their journeys with the same insight I've been receiving from Source. Divine Source is loving, and it is amazing to feel the pure love of Source when we love ourselves. It is the energy that is in everything. We are a part of it but may not be aware of it. Since like attracts like when we are aware of the love of self, we get to be in alignment with the love of Source. That is profound and achievable.

I trust the process that the universe will always engage in a partnership to help us all and appreciate the partnership the universe bestows upon me to help all who seek help. As I serve as a vibration-ship, a conduit to others, I'm fully aware that the work is between my clients and Source. I get to help make that connection while we engage in our conversation and start receiving the downloads from the Source of knowledge.

Although, I bring in the same concept to everyone, the information comes in at the unique frequency of the person I'm working with. It is gratifying to hear myself talk as I translate the information. It helps me learn along with it. I suggest to my clients to open up their heart to listen and if they resonate with any information; I strongly suggest that they own it, claim it, embody it and accept their truth in love and light.

This is a beautiful gift we can give to ourselves leading to self-healing and find a permanent solution. We need to make changes in the belief systems that are not ours and especially when they are not from the light. We must be able to discern the difference and it is important to know all the options that are available to us and utilize our freewill making the decisions based on our truth, not from programming or deception of others. This is how my work has a very high percentage of success because when people have the awareness of what needs to be changed and know what must be changed and are committed to that change, anything is possible when that shift of consciousness takes place. Even the sky is no longer a limit after that.

When the universe and I conduct sessions to help people, I ask clients to free up their entire day so we can put all of our focus, attention and effort into it. I do not set up a time limit for the session because I want to give one thousand percent of myself to help my clients achieve their goals for self-healing and ascending to a higher vibration and beyond. How long each session takes depends on the complexity of each individual. The more complexity, the longer the session will be. I notice that the session is short when working with someone who is willing and ready to make all the necessary changes in their thought forms and belief systems that do serve them well. Sometimes in a few hours we are done with lasting effects and I thank them for making those fine choices for themselves.

On the other hand, the people who resist changes may have a resisting habit, a resistance to their own growth, and our sessions could carry on for several hours until we achieve the ultimate goal. There were times when we put so much work into it, but the conscious mind still interfered and did not allow the process of letting go of old belief systems to take place, so they still feel stuck. In this case, we would have to do another session. It has only happened on rare occasions. Like I mentioned earlier, this work to help people is not a band-aid, it is a permanent solution. Changing the belief system will change the entire reality in our creation of life experiences.

I always put my all in to helping everyone, and when they put their all in, magical things can happen. I'm grateful for the knowledge that Dolores bestowed upon us and appreciate her loving kindness and her pure intention. She gave us her personal touch with her advanced teaching. It has been continuously helping to build my skill and confidence. I am extremely grateful for being a part of her network in helping humanity with Quantum Healing and the bonus I receive in doing it. I get to experience more phenomenal encounters that ring true for me from giving sessions.

I've learned that QHHT and DVM are alike in the way that each method helps people make the connection to the Higher Self, the Source of knowledge that lies within us. This source is connected to The Great Center, the original life force energy of the frequency signal. They are a part of us all because they are us! I use the word 'they' because they are a collective consciousness consisting of subconscious, super conscious and supreme consciousness. This is a part of the inner guidance that we always have, but some of us may not be aware of it. That's why it is important that we listen and learn and become more aware of this gift.

We all have this same inner guidance that is all loving. This is our best Self that always has our best interests in mind. We can call them the Higher Self, and keep in mind the Higher Self is not singular. The Higher Self is at one with the universe, a part of the same center Source. They are a part of a whole. We are a part of that wholeness of ONE! And this is our true authentic self that I'm talking about! We are One with the universe and the universe works hard to get our attention. I mentioned earlier that many of us may not be aware of them at all. I wish to bring that awareness to you now that we have our best true selves that hold the divine power within us. We are a part of a quantum energy that is so huge, benevolent, powerful, loving, caring, kind, compassionate, peaceful and harmonious, and yes, this is who we truly are at our core essence. We just have to claim it, own it and allow ourselves to be one with it!

It is a satisfying and gratifying feeling for me to be practicing QHHT, and to be able to help people making that connection with the Source of Knowledge/the Higher Self, and I get to experience the pure magic of this benevolent energy regularly. I listened and learned from the guidance that my clients have brought forth during our sessions. I feel like I now have a trusted navigator to experience life with amazing insight. This has been very enlightening for me. I have witnessed so many life changing experiences that I get to see from my clients by facilitating the self-healing for them with quantum healing practice. It has been empowering to those who receive the guiding light for their journeys, and I apply the same guidance received to my own life too.

We have not been taught to have an awareness of how powerful we are and what options are available for us to choose from. We only know of the options that we were programmed to believe within the limitations of other people's belief systems. Things are changing dramatically, and it is being intensified lately in helping humanity to learn and acquire the knowledge of the authentic truth. This is why I felt compelled to share it with others. I believe in my heart that all the information I'm sharing in this book will help many people in waking up to their truth.

The knowledge that has been dormant within us can be awakened right here and right now. As I download and translate the information for others with my gift of clairaudience, the information that people resonate with becomes their tools, encouraging them to make changes essential that uniquely fit their needs. This change is not temporary. It is a permanent change if they choose it to be, and it has a life changing effect indeed. Also, it becomes a ripple effect throughout their circles. These changes will have a strong influence on those people around them. I too, get to utilize this same tool. I mentor and coach others with it at the soul level.

I started offering a Soul Coaching Session to people. This is to help them acknowledge who they are not and get to know who they really are at their core essence. It is very useful for the people who are looking for positive change in life and the ones who could use some help with it. I find it highly effective to help people this way with my gift of clairaudience, bringing in the guiding light, the knowledge from the universe that could help people find their true self and overcome life's issues.

I am a bridge helping people make a connection with the universe at the frequency level of truth. I help bring in the information that they need to know, and I guide them along showing them how to utilize it. I help people to listen to their own thoughts so they can hear themselves talk. This way they can be more aware of the thought process within the habit of thinking the thoughts that may have a negative effect in their lives. By learning this process of thought and belief awareness with a guide, it teaches an individual how to become their own guide, and a guide to others. The change can take place in that moment if they choose to do so. This change is being made from the self-acknowledgment that they've gained from listening and learning; they will be able to utilize these tools the rest of their lives.

Awareness is the key. Having an awareness helps them acknowledge the area that needs to be changed. Knowing how to make changes and what needs to be changed can be gained when they open up to listen. Choice is the most precious tool that we all have because of freewill. When we choose to make needed changes instantly, voila, lots of improvement can be done. It is the thought and the belief system that shape us so much.

And again, because thoughts become words, words become actions, actions become our own character and we are what we believe. If things are not working well, something has to change. We must change at the root cause of the problems. The root cause of the problems most of the time start from our thought process and our belief system. We can become aware of negative thought patterns and beliefs and choose to change them. You can do it. We all can do it. We can't think the same thought, talk the same talk, act the same act, stay the same character, and hold on to the same belief system and expect things to change.

As Einstein said, ***"The belief system that creates a problem, cannot solve the problem."*** When we make the decision to change and start thinking more positively and refine our belief system, our reality will start changing. I've been walking that talk myself and life has been magical for me. Many people in my inner circle have been affected and influenced by my change and the ones who are more adapted to make good changes along with me have been living life with more joy and are able to enjoy the process of getting to their destiny of whatever their hearts desire. The changes within themselves also have a strong influence on others around them. It is the gift of self that keeps on giving.

It is like being a lit candle and wherever there is light, there is no darkness. A lit candle loses nothing by lighting another candle. Light casts no shadows. It only illuminates more light. Others who are gravitated to the light would want to bring their own candles to be lit and take the light home and continue to do the same thing to others. This is how we can light up the community, create a ripple effect, and create a critical mass for the light, for love.

Now, let's imagine together that each one of us has done the self-work, making changes that truly support us and imagine how our positive changes affect people around us. Can you see how peaceful life would be for all of us? Very good feeling, right? How about this beautiful world that we live in? Imagine it on a larger scale now. Imagine, seeing the domino effects with the positive changes toward others throughout the globe. Could you see what I see? Imagine seeing a huge difference that we can make in this beautiful world.

Are you ready to make some great changes in your life? Let's do it together! I have witnessed it within my own circle with the changes I have made within me. I get to see the positive changes in my family and friends. The ones who are ready to make changes and are willing to accept changes get the most out of it. Those who are not open to it may not have any effect and that is okay too. We all have freewill. We cannot change others, although we can change ourselves, and that will influence others like the metaphor of being a lit candle.

Start from releasing the old thought patterns that do not serve us well and bring in the new way of thinking that energizes and uplifts our spirit. This is the gift that I wish to give to everyone. I enjoy coaching people and helping them make changes at the soul level and I help them claim their divine light, the very same way that I've claimed mine. It is very gratifying to see positive changes in others as they choose it. That reality can be yours too if you listen and learn from your inner guidance. How do we listen so we can learn? Very simple! Just practice a daily meditation. I always suggest to people that they set up a priority in life and do 3 things every single day,

meditate, meditate and meditate because when we meditate, it has been scientifically proven that our brainwaves slow down. At those moments we take our conscious mind to the Alpha level, the first altered state of consciousness.

At this point we tap into our pineal gland and activate the right side of the brain where our wisdom resides. When we meditate, we are in silent mode and when we are not thinking we get to listen to the wisdom within us. I always ask my clients to meditate daily prior to our sessions, because I believe that it will enhance the ability to connect with the Higher Self, the part of self that has an in-depth knowledge. This definitely enhances the ability to bring out the wisdom. We all can use more wisdom in our life. Wisdom is the common sense that is not so common. Not many people have common sense because of a lack of connection to the wisdom self in the right brain. When we practice a daily meditation, we increase our common sense and gain great wisdom, raising the intuition that is the inner knowing, the inner guidance that we should have. Give a gift to yourself - - meditate daily. It is free. You can do it anywhere and anytime. I will help you understand it in depth in my next chapter on The Higher Vision of Meditation.

We all can tap into this knowledge, but we must reconnect and stay connected. To reconnect and stay connected can be quite easy and it only takes a desire to do so. With the quantum healing hypnosis that I do, it is important to help my clients make the connection with the Higher Self to receive the self-healing and to receive some of the answers that they may have. Again, this is why I ask my clients to practice a daily meditation. Meditation enhances their ability to go under hypnosis and tap into the alpha or theta level, because hypnosis is very similar to meditation. It is a natural state to step into the alpha or theta levels, while the beta is stepping aside.

When we make that connection with the Source of knowledge within, the sky is no longer the limit! We can heal ourselves and when we maintain that state of mind, the healing is permanent. If we do not allow ourselves to slip back into the negative pattern and bring back the bad habits, we are on the way to achieve the ultimate goal, that is to find joy in life! Joy is permanent! It is a state of mind. Joy fills us with complete happiness. Happiness is only temporary. We may be happy now, but not happy later. We will always be happy if we are in the state of joy! When we shift our beliefs and thoughts to positive patterns it prepares us to live in joy. That is why becoming aware of our own thoughts and beliefs is so critical. I will dedicate the next chapter to help you innerstand the art and science of meditation at a deeper level.

Chapter Three:
The Higher Vision of Meditation

Do you meditate daily? If not, would you like to give it a try? Or if you already do so, you may want to make it your priority after you read all these facts from a scientific point of view and learn about the art of meditation that I will present to you. Come, let me show you why I believe it is important that you put meditation into your daily practice if you have not already done so. Meditation is free and you can practice it at anytime and anywhere; while you are siting, standing, walking, doing something or doing nothing. There are many ways to meditate, and there is no right or wrong way to do it.

I believe that each method serves the same purpose and that is to turn us away from our busy chattering mind, the busy mind that has a habit of thinking all the time. I wish to show you a few different ways to meditate. All of them have been working well for me and I truly appreciate the simplicity of these practices as well! My intention is to help you find this treasure inside of you and I wish to help you become more aware of its benefits. Meditation is natural and organic. Its process has unlimited benefits. It also plays an important role in bridging us to our Higher wisdom. Meditation helps us connect to the collective universal consciousness that is very wise and very loving.

I would like to describe some of the science behind meditation and I want to make it simple for you. I believe it is important to have a good understanding of how it works and why it works. Through my own experiences I know for sure that it does work!

We operate at 4 levels of consciousness: (1) Beta, (2) Alpha, (3) Theta and (4) Delta on a daily basis.

We go in and out of these 4 levels every single day at least twice a day; from Beta, the waking moment, to Alpha, the first altered state of consciousness, to Theta, a deeper level of consciousness and to Delta, the sleep mode when we fall asleep. We wake up from Delta, to Theta, to Alpha and back to Beta as we awaken each day. Also, we go in and out, back and forth between Beta and Alpha every 60 seconds and may not be aware of it.

Level of Consciousness	Description
(1) Beta	Alert conscious intellectual focus. Left brain focused. Lower consciousness of the mind and ego.
(2) Alpha	The first altered state of consciousness. Right brain focused. Bridges the gap between our conscious thinking and subconscious mind. A source of deep wisdom.
(3) Theta	Deep state of consciousness. Deep connection to inner knowing.
(4) Delta	Deepest level of relaxation and restoration. Deepest level of sleep and rejuvenation.

Beta is the alert conscious level of the mind. In Beta we are in our conscious thought; logical thinking, critical thinking, writing, reading, socializing and other modes of being. This is the intellectual conscious level of the mind. We learn intellectually from the left side of the brain. This is a lower conscious level of the brain. We may call it the ego, the lower self. The ego thinks a lot and of course, it thinks it knows everything too. The left brain is always too busy thinking and does not listen. If those thoughts are negative and it becomes a habit of thinking negative thoughts, imagine how those thoughts could affect us mentally and emotionally.

The stress hormones that our body produces each time we have a negative thought are accepted by the heart, turning into emotion and feeling that can greatly destroy the healthy cells in the body. This is how we make ourselves sick. When stress hormones are being accumulated over time, the most vulnerable organ will take the greatest toll. When it does not function properly anymore, the organ nearby will jump in to assist, as was the case with my liver episode. My gallbladder had to jump in to help out until both organs could not handle it anymore. That was when the physical manifestation occurred which was almost too late to handle.

The severity of my health issue was my own creation generated by my feeling of being unworthy of love, my self-esteem and self-confidence were low. I kept replaying in my mind that I was a victim and kept sabotaging myself toward illness. Our bodies respond to every emotion and emotion turns into feeling. Feeling is a powerful energy within us. It can build us up or break us down depending on the severity of the emotion that our heart accepts.

In my case, I had a bad habit of thinking unkind thoughts about myself and when the heart accepted those thoughts, the emotion it received were filled with feelings of hurt and pain. Every time this happened my body responded naturally as it programmed, producing stress hormones and releasing adrenaline which in excess destroys healthy cells in the body. It accumulated overtime until my system became out of balance and progressed from dis-ease into disease.

The lack of self-realization, lack of self-awareness and lack of self-acknowledgement kept me in a loop, and I kept repeating those negative thoughts like a broken record. My mode of thinking made it feel like everything that everyone ever did or said to me in life which hurt me was still happening in every moment. It was a repeating loop of pain, constantly draining me. Luckily, I made a bold move by practicing using my right brain to tap into the Alpha level just in time to combat stress. It literally saved my life. Again, I learned from that experience and created positive thought patterns and belief systems as a result. We can all do the same thing if we choose.

Learning to quiet the mind alone was extremely helpful. My ego, the lower self, did not have the same loud voice as it did before, so its power was lessened. At the beginning, when I only practiced it when I needed it, the lower self, had an opportunity to steal the moments back and I would go back into a habit of thinking the negative thoughts when unaware. After my hospital stay, I rediscovered the importance of meditation practice, and I decided to make it my priority to practice it in a daily routine, the change in me was phenomenal.

Once I did that, it felt like my stress level was lower as I gave less power to the chattering mind. Ever since then it became my top priority to tame the lower mind and enhance my ability to be in the Alpha level to keep me more balanced and centered. My intention is to bring the Alpha brain wave level to your awareness so that you can be more balanced and centered now, so that you do not have to go through dis-ease in order to innerstand its importance. I want to help you create the life that you desire, filled with an abundance of love, peace and joy.

Let's get into that amazing Alpha level of consciousness now. This is the first altered state of consciousness. This frequency level bridges the gap between our conscious thinking and subconscious mind. It brings calmness, peace and harmony, because it promotes deep relaxation. We are in this Alpha stage of the mind during meditation, listening to music, reading good books, daydreaming, spending time in nature and doing simple activities. Alpha brain waves are slower than beta brain waves and what's so amazing about them is that they help us make a connection with our right brain through the pineal gland. When we make this connection, the pineal gland actively produces more melatonin and serotonin. As we become restful, we activate more use of the right brain. This side of our brain is our genius side, the spiritual side. The side that is full of wisdom.

All the enlightened ones became enlightened by practicing meditation and taking their brain waves to this Alpha level to experience Self-healing, Stress release, Heightened Intuition, Compassion, Empathy, and Enhanced Creative Manifestation. Enlightened or enlightenment means well informed, aware, developed, knowledgeable, wise, refined, sophisticated. This is the reason why we need to meditate, so our right brain will be more active, so we can be more enlightened. We get to reconnect and stay connected with the Higher Self, the Divine Source within. This is the intelligent side of the brain. Intelligence means information, knowing. It is the wisdom that lies within us. Wisdom is a common sense, a sense that is not very common. Common sense is really the innate wisdom of the heart. Very few people have it because we do not often tap into it.

When we meditate, our brain waves are at the Alpha level, the first altered state of consciousness, and when we meditate regularly, we promote a good feeling leading to positive thinking. When we have peace and harmony it promotes more joy; the body releases endorphins, dopamine and serotonin to strengthen healthy cells in the body. More heathy cells being regenerated enhances our ability to self-heal. Our body has an amazing ability to replenish healthy cells improving vital energy to self-heal, but we have to enhance our ability to naturally generate that. Practice being in resonance with the Alpha level will do just that.

A deeper level than Alpha is Theta. Theta brain waves are even slower than Alpha, and this is when we are in a very deep state, connecting with real experiences at a deeper level of consciousness. If we can tap into a Theta level of consciousness during meditation, phenomenal experiences can be brought forth to us from deep inner knowing, the innate wisdom of the heart, the soul, the Higher Self, Source; all connected as one.

Delta is the slowest brain wave and it provides the deepest level of relaxation and restoration healing sleep happens at this level for the physical body. We feel completely replenished and rejuvenated after we have a good night's sleep.

It is important to talk more about the alpha level. As I mentioned to you earlier this is the level at which the connection between the conscious mind and the subconscious mind is naturally taking place. As the brain slows down during meditation, we are tapping into the pineal gland. At this point, the pineal gland activates the right side of the brain and the collective consciousness that is filled with wisdom. This is our genius side, the spiritual, peaceful side. The side that is filled with love, peace, harmony and wisdom.

Many geniuses say they received their inspiration for their great art, music, inventions, theories and ideas from their dreams. When we sleep, we all go into the Alpha, Theta and Delta brainwave states. These brainwave states awaken our hearts, our wisdom, and our creativity. We can access that same awareness through meditation.

Let me explain to you more in depth about the difference between the left and right brain and how they operate. Our mind is in the brain. The brain has two sides, the left and the right, which function differently. As I mentioned earlier, the left brain is the intellect. We use this side of the brain to reason logically. It operates at a lower level of consciousness. It performs the ego functioning of the brain. It thinks a lot and it thinks it knows everything. When it doesn't know, it becomes frustrated and angry. It creates the feelings of fear of the unknown, always working on questions of what if, and what if not? The left brain needs to rest. It needs to have less action. It is not a good leader so we shouldn't allow it to navigate us too much in life and the beauty is, we can definitely do something about it. I'm going to show you how to calm the mind in a little bit.

Let's talk about the other half of the brain, in the right side. This is the intelligent side of the brain, the collective version of the subconscious, superconscious, and supreme consciousness of self. Intelligence means information. Information gains knowledge. Knowledge is wisdom. This right side of the brain operates at a higher level of consciousness with loving thoughts, kindness, compassion, joy, peace, harmony and all the good feelings people wish for. It is much more pleasant for the mind to be connected with the right side of the brain and true consciousness.

All of those positive energies and frequencies I mentioned are available to us when we tap into it. Now, let's get to the good part about the function of the left and right sides of our brains. Imagine having a habit of the left brain being more active than the right side, where the power is being given mostly to the ego. The ego gets frustrated easily and will throw tantrums like a two-year-old sometimes does. The ego gets angry at others and itself. That is a totally draining and an unproductive way to be. Bad decisions will be made under that kind of influence. We need to use the right brain more often, it has control over the loving heart which is kind and caring. With greater wisdom we can prevent the two-year old ego from throwing tantrums.

By the way, the left brain has control over the right side of the body and the right brain has control over the left side of the body. That is why two-thirds of our hearts are in the left side of the body. The collective consciousness has control of the heart that is all about love and compassion. This is another reason why we need to meditate, so we can make the connection with the loving heart.

We can do it by simply finding the time to meditate daily. Just simply include meditation in your daily life. Practicing it a few minutes a day is still better than not doing it at all. We activate the ability to access more wisdom, and of course, the more we meditate, the greater the accumulation of the wisdom we will have. Daily doses of wisdom will keep the chattering mind away. Perhaps we could think less and not waste any energy thinking thoughts that create disharmony. We can live life more productively with an awareness of our thought processes and utilize our freewill to choose happier thoughts - - having a better relationship with everyone, becoming more energized.

Activating the right brain brings out our ability to be more aware of our own thought processes. If we don't like our thoughts, we can change them within 3 seconds. Try it and you will be amazed how easy and effective it is. We will be able to make changes that are more complementary to us and more supportive to us by activating the use of the right side of the brain. It is already there and always available. These are the pure intuitive thoughts that do not need filtering. We become more aware of our thoughts as wisdom arises. It is essential to have awareness of our thoughts. Again, it is critical to remember that thoughts become words, words become actions, actions become our character and we are what we believe! As we believe, we become! We will create our reality based on our belief systems. If things are not working well in our lives, we will need to change our belief system to change our reality.

Many of us may not be aware that social standards, environment, upbringing and life experiences have been programmed into our belief system. These beliefs may cause more harm than good to us because we will be living our lives under the rules of others - - the rules that set up limitations and stop the flow of life. With the limitations established by the rules of others, it makes us feel like we are being judged because we are not following these external standards and we can become fearful of being rejected as well. If you are not following your own rules, then you are likely unconsciously following the rules others have taught you to follow.

Living life under the influence of fear and judgement will create thoughts that are often negative. As we keep thinking negative thoughts and our hearts accept them, we create emotions that are not in alignment with our true self, the Higher Self. When negative emotions are accumulated and become our emotional baggage, we carry them with us and drag them into every relationship. When we hold on to the belief systems that are not supporting us well, it feels like we are being dragged down and not able to function at our best.

It is harder to be happy and loving when we are carrying a heavy load of emotional baggage. It is harder to carry on a good relationship with someone when we drag along emotional baggage into any relationship. It takes more energy and eventually will exhaust us to the point that we can no longer keep it going. It feels like we just have much less to give. Also, when our belief system is misaligned, our thought processes will be negative and becomes destructive to self. We then slowly erode from the inside.

On the other hand, when we practice meditation, we start tapping into the powerful collective side of the brain. When we activate more use of it, we have the wisdom to help us thrive throughout life. We are much calmer and have the inner peace that balances our own body, mind and soul. And this is when we become more and more aware of our thoughts. We have the awareness that we need to catch our thoughts. If we do not like those thoughts, we can change them within 3 seconds.

Yes, it takes only 3 seconds to change our thought processes from negative to be positive. With our intention we can add those 3 seconds of awareness of our thoughts to our daily lives. It can make a huge difference in how we live our lives and coexist with others. It can change the dynamics in every relationship that we have and increase the kindness and compassion we express towards one another. Our thoughts are integral parts of every loving relationship we have, whether as a couple, family, friends, siblings, coworkers or any other relationship. It is also important to remember when you notice a thought or belief you don't like within 3 seconds you can change or replace or just let go of it. If you observe it, don't like it, but let it remain, it will not change.

Awareness of negative thought patterns and beliefs is not enough. We have to go one step further and choose to shift negative or limiting thoughts and beliefs. Then we can choose to transform them into positive, loving ones that allow us to thrive in life where we eventually experience love and joy every day.

The benefits from practicing meditation are limitless. They include stress reduction, and gently relaxing of the nervous system, which helps us calm our nerves and release muscle tension which helps relieve pain, even PMS pain. It decreases mood swings, increases creativity and awareness, improves quality of sleep and much more. With restful, good quality sleep, we will need less sleep, but will have more energy. Meditation also aids in losing weight, and as you become more energized, you will be able to increase your physical activity. The body's immunity will be increased as it boosts Serotonin, Endorphins, Dopamine and Oxytocin.

Serotonin is being released naturally when we are at peace and in harmony without thoughts. Endorphins are being produced by the central nervous system from various sources within the body. Meditation, exercise, laughter, music, eating chocolate, singing, dancing, writing, drawing, painting, crafting, gardening and many other activities promote production of Endorphins in the body because we are happy when doing those activities.

Just doing more of what we love, anything that brings us joy enhances the production of Endorphins. Dopamine plays important roles in the brain and body. It is a reward system that can help lower blood pressure and lower heart rate. It is an organic chemical produced from feeling satisfied. Oxytocin is a powerful hormone in the brain. It is the love hormone produced organically when we are in love, joyful, or feeling compassion and gratitude.

As our immune system becomes strengthened, it produces increased levels of super-antioxidants, preventing illness or speeding up healing, lowering blood pressure, lowering respiratory rate, causing better breathing, better circulation, contributing to having more patience and peace of mind, slowing down aging, and leading to increased longevity. Enhancing our immune system increases brain development, willpower to beat addiction, improves memory, self-confidence and creativity.

This whole brain synchronization can even raise IQ, by balancing the function of both sides of the brain. Both intellect and wisdom are synchronizing and integrating more harmoniously. This is the kind of wisdom that I was talking about earlier. When wisdom rises, it will increase our connection to our own spirit and leads us to having greater power of introspection, and an increase in empathy and allows us to have a broader and deeper perspective.

There is a change in attitude that will enhance our ability to let go and forgive. The ability to let go and to forgive is something I feel that lots of people have a hard time doing. When we make a decision to forgive and commit to do so, we get to set ourselves free,

free from any burden of carrying baggage that weighs us down more and more every day. Remember that when we are able to let go, we navigate through life a whole lot lighter and when we forgive, we are not doing it for others as much as we are doing it for ourselves. The main purpose of forgiveness is to set us free, free from all the burdens and just be free! These are only some of the benefits we can have directly from adapting meditation into our daily routine.

I am thinking about the story that happened in my homeland, Thailand in 2018 that made international news for several weeks and was still the most talked about story for months to come. I'm sure most of you have heard about it. It was about the 12 young soccer players and their coach that were trapped for many days two and a half miles inside a cave, "Tham Luang Nang Non" in northern Thailand.

This incredible situation received attention from people all over the world. Media all over the globe covered the story 24/7. We all had the same intention during that time and that intention was to find them and find them alive. We were not sure if that would be the case then. This became a focus of people worldwide. Different experts from everywhere wanted to do what they could do and help with their expertise. Ninety divers from 22 countries became involved, tens of thousands of people with different expertise pulled together as one unit.

This event really made an impact on humanity and demonstrated the beauty of cooperation within mankind that brought out the best in one another. I would also like to bring to your attention, using this event as an example, how our subject of meditation relates to the outcome of the story. I want to show you how much meditation benefited those 13 people in the caves. The coach was able to handle the situation amazingly well. He utilized meditation skill he learned during his childhood while being raised by Buddhist monks. The coach taught the boys meditation techniques that obviously helped them to endure this life-threatening crisis. As the boys meditated during their long stay in the cave, they were able to stay calm and that allowed them to conserve their energy which would be needed to sustain them for the deprivation they experienced during their long confinement.

Meditation lessened their fear while trapped in the pitch-black environment, and that prevented them from panicking. They had no food and could only drink cave water to survive. Meditation was also very helpful for controlling their hunger. The coach helped them get through this crisis with what he knew and what he knew happened to be the most valuable knowledge that one can have. From my own personal experience with Vipassana

Meditation, I can relate to how the coach was successful in assisting them with his skill by helping them learn how to tap into the altered state of consciousness and ultimately have the control that was needed during this major crisis.

The goal was to locate these 12 boys and their coach. Thousands of people became involved from all over the world. Everybody focused on one goal and united as one during that time. They weren't even sure that the soccer team and their coach would be alive when they found them. All thirteen people had the strength that was needed to overcome their desperate situation. They survived and made it out of the cave! So, the impossible mission was possible for the first time in human history.

This demonstrates a multiple team effort that led to success. Every team put everything they had into searching and rescuing. But if the boys and their coach could not have cooperated by handling the major crisis in flow, you can imagine how the process of getting them out would have turned out instead. Imagine how difficult the situation was even for the highly skilled divers to dive in those treacherous conditions. The boys had no skills, some couldn't even swim and they only received basic training from the diver team. What the boys needed to do was to stay calm the entire time under water and trust the process. They did!

Let's be realistic! If they did not have a chance to learn meditation and practice calmness during those 9 days in a dark cave with their coach, would they have survived? Just one wrong move could have made the crisis even worse. It was a good thing that there was a combination of meditation skills and anti-anxiety drugs that helped them exit the cave for the rescue to be successful. And boy! They all were heroes. I take my hat off and bow to all that were involved in the rescue. This story is a very good example of how meditation can help with the control of one's state of mind in any situation. This time it kept them alive and well. Well, have you been inspired to meditate more now? I believe so. See if you can make it your daily priority.

Okay, let me get into how to do it now. As I mentioned earlier there are many different ways to meditate. It is like the many flavors of ice-cream. When you find the one that you enjoy the most, you may have a craving and want to eat it more often. Meditation and other good habits can be like that. When we find the natural way of doing it for us, it will take no effort. Being in that state of mind is the key. Be in the flow with our body, mind and soul. Be in a state of peace and harmony. Make it feel like you are enjoying your ice-cream and always look forward to having more of it.

Here is one of the meditation practices that I want to show you which is very simple to put in your daily routine whether you are already a meditator or a newbie. You can give this a try every morning and every night with simplicity. Again, I need to describe the basic foundation of the 4 levels of consciousness that we go through every day: (1) beta to (2) alpha to (3) theta and to (4) delta to sleep. Then we wake up from delta to theta to alpha and back to beta to be awake every day. When we wake up in the morning, we wake up from delta to theta and to alpha but not to beta immediately, our body is still in a very relaxed state. So, while we are still at this alpha level of consciousness, we can allow ourselves to stay in bed for a little bit longer. Well, some of you already like that idea, right? We are still in that meditative level of the alpha state of consciousness, we are not back into our daily morning routine in the beta level yet.

By the way, just make sure that you give yourself enough time to do this because you don't want to feel rushed or concerned about getting out of bed sooner. You want to be in the zone of being in the moment. Find the way that is most suitable for you to manage that time in the morning. Start your day by giving this meditation practice as a gift to yourself. It is ME time that you deserve. Being in a restful state of mind, practice mindfulness and activate your awareness before you start your day. It is an awesome way to start your day with peace and harmony and feeling more balanced and centered. This way will definitely help you become more equipped for any surprises that life may throw at you. Metaphorically, it is like preparing to make a pot of soup, you want to select your ingredients carefully. It is your soup that will nurture you, so make it a good one.

Here is how! First place your hands on your heart with your eyes closed and start taking a few deep breaths. Imagine that it is almost like you are breathing through your heart. You are getting in touch with your heart right now. Keep your mind in silence and just focus on the heartbeat. Bring your awareness to the rhythm of the beats and feel the feeling of gratitude that your heart is beating. When you get in touch with your own heart, you are in more flow and you are more connected with your true self. Heart is all about love and love is the energy of Divine Source in us. Feel the love that your heart has to offer and feel the connection with that loving heart of yours.

Next after you have created the feeling of love and gratitude, move your focus to your breath, place your awareness on your breathing pattern. Follow the pattern of your breath as you are breathing in and out naturally. Keep focusing on your breath and allow your body to sink into a deeper state of relaxation. Notice that the tension in your body is fading away. When your body relaxes, your mind relaxes and when you are more relaxed you can start placing your focus into listening to the sound of the frequency in your brain. It is the sound of the frequency inside your brain between the ears that I am referring to. If you can hear the frequency sound, place your intention on listening to the sound and turn the volume up louder. Keep listening to the sound. This is the sound of the frequency of Divine Source within you. Focus on that sound and allow your breath to slow down, breathe gently in and out naturally.

Thinking no thoughts is the key! Just enjoy listening to the frequency of your inner self and enjoy the relaxation. Feel that good feeling and take the time to enjoy the rhythm that slow breathing brings to you. If you have a habit of thinking, it is okay. Just be kind to yourself. Do not get frustrated and just gently bring your focus back to listening to the sound of frequency as many times as you need to. It is a part of practicing awareness. It is normal. When you are more aware of your thinking habits, and start adapting, it will become easier to practice and let your mind rest.

Yes, at the beginning of this practice some of your mind may be chattering and that is okay. Use your practice of awareness to notice if you are thinking, then gently switch it back to being in silent mode if you do not hear the frequency. Staying in the silent mode is the key. Whatever works for you. Meditation is not about doing. It is about being. Being in the silent mode to quiet your mind without distraction from any thought is the key. Make sure that you do not get frustrated and just be in flow with it. Somedays, it may be more natural to you than others. Just put no effort into it. Don't try to force yourself into being. Remember to just be because being is a state of mind. It is opposite from doing or trying.

Enjoy following the rhythm of your heart beats. Some of you may hear the beats which again is an extra bonus. Keep listening and tune into it completely. Just allow yourself to learn to get in touch with your own heart to make a connection with your loving self, your soul in your spirit of Divine Source, the Higher Self.

Enjoy having your awareness of your breath. Breath is the life force that comes from Source energy that creates life, so it is the life force energy that created you and it is a part of you. The frequency is the vibration of the higher wisdom, the Higher Self in you. The heart is all about love, so it is the same love that the life force energy and frequency that are a part of you. You can practice fine tuning to see which one of the three (heartbeats, breath or frequency) you are most connected with and be one with it. Some may like tuning to all three and that is even more powerful. Have fun with it. There is no right or wrong way to practice meditation. Focusing your awareness on your heartbeats, breath, or frequency helps bring you into the alpha brainwave state. Once you are in a state of being where your mind is quiet, you can just be and let your mind focus more softly. Just BE is the key!

You can meditate at the end of the day too. When you are comfortable in bed at the end of the day, your breath naturally slows down and is ready to snooze off. You are getting ready to go from beta, into alpha, to theta before you get into the delta state to sleep. Mindfully enjoy the relaxing feeling of your body and allow your mind to relax as well. Feel yourself releasing tension in your muscles, release and let go from taking your long deep breaths and slowly letting go of tension with every breath. Start listening to the sound of the frequency within you and remember to turn up the volume if you can hear it and sink into alpha level. This technique is helpful, conditioning your mind to be busy listening instead of being busy thinking.

By this time your body and your mind are relaxed, you will doze off into theta before going into sleep mode in delta. It is so natural and this way you will be able to release stress and prepare the body to get a restful night of sleep. You will wake up fresh, having a good feeling in the morning. And guess what? You never have to stop having the good feelings because you can enjoy practicing meditation before you get out of bed again the next morning. Is this simple enough for you? I know, right? It works for me too!

Please remember that some of you may not hear the frequency right away and this is fine. Just practice focusing on your breathing. This will already do much good and as you become more in sync with your inner self, everything will become more natural and at ease. Again, keep in mind that meditation is about being, not about doing or trying. The less effort, the easier and more effective meditation will be. Make it simple and let it flow.

Now you can slowly add meditation into your daily routine. Once you get the meditation practice into a routine you will look forward to being in that state of mind more often. Now, it is the time to add more practice of Being-ness. The fact is that you can meditate at anytime, anywhere in any situation at any given moment. You can practice being mindful, observing your breath as you are breathing in and out, deepening and slowing the breath down as you are doing your chores, taking a bath, a shower, a walk or just sitting and having restful moments during the day, even when waiting in a line at the store, or while you are in bed. Be creative with it. As you are focusing within, just go inward to listen to your frequency instead of thinking those thoughts.

Voila! You will become more in the flow with the universe and start making connection with your right brain that has so much wisdom. You will notice your ability to make better decisions and feel wiser. You will have better sleep patterns leading to good health and longevity. What is the difference between being wise and being smart? Wisdom comes from the heart, the Higher Self, the soul, and Divine Source. We often sense wisdom as common sense. It is what feels right, even if we cannot explain it.

Smartness comes from intellect and focuses on gaining knowledge. Intellect is connected to the ego, the lower self. It is nice to have both, so your left and right brain become more balanced, integrated and supportive of one another. Being smart and having wisdom can take us very far in life and it can bring much joy. Once we are able to claim our wisdom, who would want to give it up, right? So, this is another important reason why we need to practice meditation in our daily life.

This beautiful connection with our best true self is too precious to let it pass by. I like having this beautiful connection with Divine energy. I make sure I have time to meditate an extra 30 minutes before I see a client because it is important that I tune into the frequency signal fully so I can naturally download information for everyone. It works so well for me because I am fully committed to be of service to everyone and serve as a conduit for the universe to mankind.

Do you want to have joy in your life? Are you willing to make changes that will bring you joy? If so, start practicing meditation regularly! Create a beautiful garden in your heart and your mind and nurture it with love, peace, harmony and joy that you can tap into with practice. It is your personal sanctuary that is yours forever. Meditation is like weeding the garden. You get to weed out any unwanted weeds that decrease the beauty of your garden. You need to do it regularly and water it with kindness and compassion. Your inner garden is worth caring for. You are worth caring for. Give that gift to yourself and thank yourself for being a good caretaker of your garden.

I posted multiple videos to help people practice a guided meditation with me on my YouTube channel: Patti Intoranat. One of them is my original, a 5 minute-meditation, which you can also find on my website to help you develop your practice. The title of this video is, "A Guided Daily Meditation for You[3]." Make sure to check it out and try it, okay? That website is:
www.hypnosisphenomenon.com

---

[3] Direct link to the 5 minutes meditation on my website http://www.hypnosisphenomenon.com/preparing-for-qhht-session

Once you reach this link, scroll down to the video, then click on the video to play it. It is within the "Preparing for QHHT Session" tab on my website. Enjoy it and remember to JUST BE! Be in joy! Be in peace! Be in harmony! In the following chapter I would like to take you to the next step towards discovering the power within your mind after you have made the connection with your best self through the daily practice of meditation.

Chapter Four:
The Higher Vision
of the Power of the Mind

I would like to help you in bringing an awareness to the magical power of the mind. I want to help you build it up to the point that you can use the Divine power within you to work on self-healing. We all have the same opportunity to tap into this power. We need to make a conscious choice to utilize it to make changes in our lives. I have a few real-life stories to share with you, so you can relate to the experiences showing how powerful our minds are. My intention is to show you and even perhaps to give you proof that we can really make major changes in life and improve our lives every day in every-way. We can prevent illnesses and even heal ourselves with the power of the mind as we utilize it and allow it to happen.

The Soul Coaching and Quantum Healing Hypnosis Technique work that I do has allowed me to experience so many expected and unexpected possibilities that it is hard for me to describe them all in words. I've learned that just because we cannot witness something as existing, does not mean it does not exist. I have learned so much from each QHHT session as I downloaded information from the Source of knowledge during our pre-hypnosis talk, (and later on from the answers that the Higher Self bestowed upon us during hypnosis), This way my clients get to hear themselves talk as I engage in our conversation as a conduit between my clients and the universe.

As I'm listening to the client's story during our pre-hypnosis talk, the spoken words represent the frequency of their thought processes. This is the time when I serve as a conduit to the client by bringing in guidance that the Source of Knowledge has to offer. I utilize my gift of clairaudience listening to the frequency as I download it and translate it into words for the client. Again, **thoughts become words, words become actions, actions become our character and we are what we believe.** When the client hears himself or herself talk, awareness is rising on the focus of the thought process behind their words. Self-acknowledgment is taking place at that moment.

This moment becomes critical. Self-awareness is taking place and the client is more ready to make changes with clarity. Having the clarity of what needs to be changed and knowing what kind of change is needed can be a life changing experience by itself. When the thought process is more refined, the spoken words are more refined, the actions are more refined, the character is more refined and when the belief systems are more refined, the reality is changing along that same path of change.

I've come across people who feel compelled to make major changes in their lives, feeling trapped and even hopeless to the point that it manifested in physical form causing fatigue. Some of the clients have multiple health issues by the time they've found me. They are not aware of the power of the mind and how they can make themselves ill. On the other hand, they can make themselves well too. It is the same mind that can either break them or build them up. The mind is like the rudder on a ship or steering wheel on a car that steers our energy.

Luckily, we can access the Higher Self as a GPS system that points us in the right direction. All we need to do is reconnect and stay connected with the Higher Self, the collective consciousness in our right brain, and stay connected by simply practicing a daily meditation. Most importantly, we have to listen and trust our inner guidance. The Higher Self, our Divine Source within is truly loving and always has our best interests in mind. It is the lower self, the ego in us that may not want to listen.

Every time we have a negative thought that our hearts accepts, it turns into emotion that then turns into a feeling, then our body's natural response is to release stress hormones into the body. It produces adrenaline, and other stress hormones from the energy of that negative thought that goes into the body. The stress hormones destroy healthy cells in the body. The most vulnerable parts of the body that are already weakened will take the most beating. This is how our dis-ease turns into disease. It does not happen overnight. The dis-ease creates disease over time, and eventually, the body's physical symptom(s) present themselves to get our attention.

When one organ becomes imbalanced, a supporting organ jumps in to assist and when the pattern of negative feelings stills persists, dis-ease multiplies and causes illness. Just like the experience that I had with my liver. By the time I found out about my liver issue, my gallbladder was already filled with stones because the liver could not effectively perform its task as a filtering system anymore, my gallbladder had to jump in to help out my liver. Neither one of them could handle the work load that stress hormones kept producing in the system. Apparently, both my liver and gallbladder started crashing down at the same time.

The severity of the health issue depends on how long the underlying emotional issue has been there. We must stop the dis-ease, the stress before it turns into a disease. Stop the discomfort before it turns into pain. Meditation combined with the powerful mind is a way to prevent it from happening. This is how we learn to be in touch with the body, and to make a connection with the mind and the spirit. If the body is already out of balance, practicing meditation and learning to shift your focus to a new way of being with a more positive mind set can help bring back the balance and ease you back to wellness.

Imagine that we are consciously aware of our thoughts and ready to make changes that we have control over. Our dynamic of body functions operates the same with every thought that the heart accepts. Thoughts become emotions and emotions turn into feelings. We can choose to create a new habit of thinking positive thoughts that will create feelings of love, peace, joy and harmony. The same mind that was once an enemy to the body can become its healer and guide. The body's natural response is to release endorphins, dopamine and serotonin that will rejuvenate, regenerate and strengthen the cells in the body. The more good feelings we create, the healthier we become. Everyone knows we can accumulate stress, but we can also accumulate relaxation, rejuvenation, and positive light energy.

This is a true story that I had an opportunity to be a part of through a new experience five years ago. A person who had 18 health issues came for a session with her two adult children. As her children were dropping her off, they asked me genuinely about my work and how it could help their mom. I invited them to stay for a little bit and I ended up talking to them for a couple hours to help them understand how I help people to help themselves through the work I do. My intention was to comfort the family and I wanted to explain how we can simply heal ourselves with the power of the mind and the power of belief that we have. I noticed that the son listened attentively, and his eyes were on me the whole time. After we were done with that talk, I asked them to go back home, since they live locally and to wait until I was done helping their mom; and they could come pick her up afterwards.

I spent at least 6 more hours with the mom to help her work on her self-healing after her kids went home, but she was still stuck because of her strong belief system that she was accustomed to, even though it did not serve her well. We agreed that she needed to have another session, which is rare because most of the time people need to have only one session spending the entire day with me, as many hours as it will take.

When her kids came back to pick her up that day, they were in awe and seemed to be extremely excited about something that had happened while they were back home. Her son said he felt the heat on his back. It was really hot, so he asked his sister to take a look at it and she saw white dots appearing in certain areas on his back. She took a picture of it to show me just in case they disappeared before they came back to see me and to pick up their mom. They even used a thermometer to check the temperature of that area in his back and compared it to the head where we normally would take the temperature of the body. The temperature was high only around that back area, but not anywhere else. The most amazing thing was that he told me he had scoliosis of the spine and his spine straightened back up to normal by itself. We were amazed by this and could not understand what had happened.

Since their mom was quite resistant to her self-healing that day, we decided to have another session to help her out. We arranged to have a surrogate session for her and invited her children to join in. By the way, this type of surrogate session is so rare, I offer it as the last resort to people that really need more help to get to the bottom of their issues to request healing from the Divine source/Source of knowledge.

Most of the people who needed to have this extra help, have already exhausted themselves trying other methods, including a QHHT session, but their conscious mind was still resisting. They no longer have a good quality of life and are willing to go the extra mile to find the solution. This was not a QHHT session. It is my other special way to be of more service to others because I always have the client's best interest in mind. The Higher Self, Source of knowledge gave me a name one day during my own surrogate session to call it "Enhanced Quantum Healing."

During our surrogate session, the Higher Self, Oneness, Source of knowledge, showed three past lives, one was for each of the family members. Due to my curious nature, just like a curious cat, I asked Source about the miracle that happened with her son's back on the day of our first session. Then Source described, *"That was to demonstrate the power of the mind and the power of belief. As the young man was listening to what you were saying Patti, you explained how powerful the mind is and how it can heal when the belief is there, he believed it with a conviction that it could be done. So, his conscious mind and subconscious mind decided to make an agreement to heal."*

By the way, I did not know that he had Scoliosis and he did not request to have any help with it either since he was used to living with it, but the miracle happened when he learned about that power and believed that it is real. Source went on to say that this is to demonstrate to his mom that the power of her negative mind got her sick so the power of her positive mind can get her well. We learned from Source that day that there were two root causes for her 18 health issues, lack of self-love and lack of self-acceptance. Source also explained to us that her daughter started having the same emotional issues of lack of self-love and lack of self-acceptance, influenced by learning the behaviors from her mother.

Fortunately, her daughter was still young. She was only 25 years old. As a result, her emotional baggage did not accumulate to the point where it would cause illness like her mother experienced. Because we were able to walk the extra mile for them, she had a chance to learn about her issues and was able to make important changes. Source said the daughter was meant to demonstrate to her mom her ability to change. She made changes in her thought process and her belief system, and therefore she was able to thrive as a result of it. I was ecstatic at this experience and I believe that this is an important story to share with my wonderful readers to demonstrate the power of the mind and the belief systems.

There is another important experience that I wish to share to demonstrate how powerful the mind is. I love telling sensational stories from the experiences that I have had with others. They speak volumes all by themselves and their magic is undeniable. This next client came for a session with a short list of questions, but a long list of requests for healing. This was an 80-year-old gentleman who drove more than 5 hours to have a session with me. Looking at him from the outside, I couldn't tell at all that he had any kind of health issues. He looked like he was in perfect health. Then once we started our talk, I realized that he had a lot of strange health issues hidden in plain sight. He said, *"I would rather try an alternative way to help myself than be put on medications the rest of my life."* Pursuing that goal was how he discovered Dolores' work and he could not wait to give it a try.

Although, we had a good session, he wasn't sure if he really had the quantum experience or if his conscious mind made it all up. When he went back home, he sent me an email stating, *"It didn't work."* He said, *"I felt like what I saw under hypnosis was all made up by my mind."* I reminded him that we are what we believe. He described that his symptoms were still there. He was so sure that it didn't work, but he really appreciated all the work I put into helping him. He told me, *"I utterly believe that it was my conscious mind that stopped me from healing."* He felt like his conscious mind was the force that blocked him from healing.

He asked me, *"Is there anything else, you can do to help me with it?"* He said, *"I cannot go on living life like this."* I told him, *"I don't give up on people."* He replied, *"I believe in you, and I am willing to do anything to be well again."* I had his best interest in mind, so

128

I offered to help him with the other work that I do with Enhanced Quantum Healing.

I offered to do a surrogate session for him to enhance the healing that he requested. This time he was much more open. We asked his Higher Self for self-healing under hypnosis session, but instead, it gave him a big surprise. The Higher Self told us that he was not sick, but because the doctor told him that he was and he believed the doctor, he started creating dis-ease in his mind and everything just escalated from there. His mind started to engage in the belief that he must have those health issues because his doctor said he had them.

He then started to create more dis-ease with his mind. He stopped living a healthy life because he started believing that he was probably too sick to do activities he enjoyed before he was diagnosed with several illnesses. He was in the Navy and enjoyed being active and liked doing things in nature like cave climbing. He said that cave climbing used to be his favorite thing to do because it gave him the best workout. He decided to stop doing that and all other activities, because he believed that he shouldn't be as active with the health issues that his doctor told him he had. He stopped doing his normal activities and just sat around the house.

As a clarification, I want to mention that the Quantum Healing Hypnosis Technique I practice is a unique modality that helps people to receive self-healing. The practitioner follows the protocol to help the client go under a deep level of hypnosis (as much as the person allows it to occur) and to make the connection with the collective mind through the right brain. Toward the end of the session the practitioner can make a request for healing and ask questions on the client's behalf. When we tap into that higher mind anything is possible; self-healing can occur, and answers are being received. His session worked along the same lines in the sense of what we could tap into, although the outcome was unique and memorable for me. It demonstrates the power of the mind and the power of belief systems. That is why this example was perfect for this chapter.

Under hypnosis, this client had a normal experience tapping into the story of a past life that was simple, then healing was requested for him. Perhaps it was so simple and easy that his mind did not want to believe what he was tapping into. This was probably the reason why he thought he made up the story during the hypnosis, because he was partially aware.

During QHHT, some people are more aware than others. How it works is that during trance, the conscious mind is still present if the person is not in Theta, as the level of consciousness remains in Alpha. It has stepped aside sitting on the sideline to observe, listen and learn from the experience. Whether the person is in the Alpha or Theta level, the Beta level is not taking part in the process. It is like the person is taking a ride but not the one that is holding the steering wheel. That was how his session went, but he was not comprehending the process, so he thought he probably made it all up. That is likely why the result created a conflict within himself. Luckily, he was aware afterwards that something definitely was happening during hypnosis, but he was having a conflict within himself. I'm glad that he was willing to cooperate more because he still believed that it could somehow work, but perhaps with extra help.

We took the next step with Enhanced Quantum Healing using Sue as a surrogate. We were able to tap into the depth of the root cause of his issue that was all in his powerful mind. Source talked to us through a surrogate and told him that he was not sick, but it was his belief that he was, and therefore, he created it with his mind. The self-healing that the Higher Self suggested was for him to stop having inner conversation with his conscious mind and start listening to the collective higher mind (Lower self vs the Higher Self!).

Furthermore, he must go back to being active, eat healthy food, drink plenty of water, meditate and go back to practicing Yoga. Most importantly, he had to stop believing that he is sick! I told him that the ball was in his court to self-heal. This time he listened! He started to make some changes by shifting his belief system to a healthier mind set and it worked magically. The following week, he sent me an email to let me know that his doctor couldn't believe that he was completely well. No more symptoms! Well, we are what we believe indeed! This story is one of many unique experiences that I was fortunate to learn through the hypnosis work that I do, and I find how simple things can be. The universe makes things so simple. It is we, humans, who have a habit of making things complicated.

What we can learn from the complexity of his experience is that at first, he totally believed his doctor that he was sick (even though he was not) and stopped living a healthy life because he already bought into believing that he must be too sick to be active. Later on, during our QHHT session, his experience was too simple, and he doubted if it could work that easily, so he did not buy into it. Then after the Enhanced Quantum healing with the surrogate, he trusted the process, resonated with Divine Source, the Higher Self and was ready to accept the truth and changed his belief to being well. Voila, he magically self-healed with his new belief system and all the symptoms magically disappeared. Even his doctor could not believe it. This story not only demonstrated the power of the mind, it proved to us that we are what believe.

Perhaps it might be useful to give you some background regarding how the discovery of my Enhanced Quantum Healing started. I would like to explain how I accidentally came across it and how I was able to utilize it to help people who needed extra help. I had an experience of my own during the time I was learning how to do a surrogate session from my late teacher, Dolores Cannon. She taught us that we could arrange for our client's friend or family member to be a hypnosis subject as a surrogate for someone. I was thrilled about it and could not wait to give it a try. When the first opportunity arose, I jumped on it.

The surrogate session was set up for a teenager who suffered a severe issue with her female organs and her mother was my client. We became friends and she offered to be a surrogate subject for her daughter to let me try out my new technique. We had a highly successful outcome. Her daughter's issues dissipated that day and we all became believers that surrogate sessions work. I became more intrigued and was hoping to have more opportunity to try it again.

Shortly after, my beloved teacher sent out the invitations to six of her students to receive a personal training for the pilot program she was to launch. This is the same program I talked about earlier which at that time was called, Recommended Dedicated Practitioners. I was ecstatic and was extremely honored to have this opportunity to become one of her proteges. I was very nervous about going to Arkansas for those 3 days of training. I felt like Dolores's bar was very high and I wanted to represent her at the highest level and put my all into it. This was a huge pressure at the time, but I really wanted to experience it. Since I had recently learned how to do a surrogate session from her during our advanced class and just had an amazing experience that blew my mind with my friend and her daughter, a light bulb went on in my head and I wondered what would happen if I try it on myself.

I persuaded my friend, Sue, to be a surrogate subject for me, and let me hypnotize her as Patti, so I could have a conversation with the Higher Self, the Oneness. My intention was to experiment to discover if I could contact the Divine Source through a surrogate subject so I could ask for help to prepare me for Arkansas. To my good fortune, she agreed to it and that was how a new unexpected phenomenal journey began. I'm glad I video recorded it with my cellphone. I was excited for the ultimate outcome and decided to select this video to send to Dolores.

One of the requirements for the training in Arkansas was to send 3 video sessions of our recent QHHT hypnosis sessions to be evaluated. I chose my own surrogate session to send to Dolores for the evaluation because I felt like I hit the jackpot and wanted to get Dolores' opinion on it. Sue went under hypnosis easily into the deepest level of trance. She could not recall any information being revealed during the two hours of our session. I felt like I just discovered my own Edgar Cayce, the sleeping prophet. We tapped into the quantum source of knowledge and experienced Oneness with Source with this endeavor. I've become dedicated to my own sessions ever since. I would do my own surrogate session with her every couple of months so I could talk to Source through her. To me, she is my "Edgar Cayce".

As I was having my conversation with Source during one of our sessions, Divine Source said to me **"You need to help your husband"**. I asked Source innocently *"How?"* because I already tried to hypnotize him 3 times and he was very resistant to it. Then Source said, **"Through a surrogate"**. *"Surrogate?"* I replied. *"Would Sue do it?"* and Source said, **"Just ask"**. Then, I asked my friend, Sue, if she would be a surrogate subject for him and she was confused about it and said, *"What? I'm your surrogate and you want me to be his surrogate too? How does it work?"* I was new at it too, so I said, *"Well, Source said that we can. Let's give it a try. Let's help him with it."* She agreed and that is how this

135

technique's use expanded through my new discovery. Source described to me that this way, we get to experience Oneness with Divine Source.

My husband is the type of person that holds on to grudges. He seems like a very angry person because of the way he handles everything in life, which is a turn off. He is this way because of some traumatic events in his life that happened because of the choices he made. His anger and sadness got the best of him and became his character, even though he has potential to be a very loving and kind man. We reminded him that we were in his allies and willing to give all the support he needed, but he still blamed himself quite harshly.

We struggled together for several years. I thrived and evolved through the situation, but he was not ready to make those changes at the time. This caused him to be characterized as someone no one enjoyed being around. He was outraged all the time and there was nothing anyone could do. Only he could make the decision to change himself. This reminded me of a joke that my son-in-law heard on the radio, *"How many therapists does it take to change a light bulb? One, but the lightbulb has to want to change itself."*

I took the opportunity to focus on myself and became enlightened through as I overcame the obstacles. I meditated and meditated even more often so I could handle being around his rage and not let it affect me as much. I had many opportunities to try new things and have found this new career that is very satisfying that has led me to do my work with great passion and feel highly productive. None of this would have happened if I did not get to experience those life situations with him. He did not see it that way then. As a result, he became more and more angry at himself and tended to take it out on his family quite often. I did not have successful hypnosis experiences with him because he would not allow it to happen.

By the way, I have to clarify that I normally have a success rate of more than 90 percent. Even though I would like it to be 100 percent, I can only facilitate self-help. I cannot force people to accept help. They have to ask for help, which invites their own connection with the Divine Source, allowing healing and transformation to take place. My husband has a habit of resisting things that can help him. I can only giggle when I see him resisting. I was excited to pursue supporting him through a surrogate session as suggested by Source during my own surrogate session with Sue.

My husband was not going to be free on the day that my friend and I were planning to get together to do the session, so he gave us permission to pursue it without him being present. We always need permission to work on someone because we cannot override their freewill. To our surprise, for some reason, he happened to be around on the scheduled day, and I was happy that he could sit in on his own surrogate session.

He was sitting next to me and observing what was going on like a fly on the wall, listening to everything that was being said. Source said, ***"It will take a few sessions working on this man because his heart is closed."*** I asked, *"How could you help him with it?"* And Source replied, ***"We are opening up his heart to receive love."*** Later during my own next surrogate session, I asked Source again, *"How could you help him at this time?"* and Source replied, ***"We are infusing the pink energy of unconditional love into his heart."*** In another surrogate session I asked Source the same questions again and 'they' replied, ***"No more blockage. He is good now."***

Since then, most of the time, he has been calm and much more pleasant to be around. It has been a few years now that we have been able to enjoy his best self and I am grateful for that experience. This personal experience of mine helped me realize that I have a new tool to help more people. A couple of years ago, I invited one of my QHHT colleagues to come for a visit from out of state. Our plan was to play in the Source field together by taking turns hypnotizing each other for the fun of it. The next day, I thought it would be even more fun to invite my friend Sue to meet up to play in Source field with us as a surrogate for us. I'm thankful that she accepted my invitation because our fun time with Source changed my colleague and her husband's lives forever.

Before my colleague flew in to visit me, her husband asked if we could help him with his anger issue. He told his wife that he was tired of being angry all the time. He did not know what to expect, but he genuinely requested help and was willing to accept the help from us. Since we had his permission, I requested help from Divine Source to support him in opening up his heart and infusing the pink energy of unconditional love into his heart the same way Source helped my husband. This happened that day between 1pm and 2pm. My friend called her husband at the end of that day to have a chat with him.

Her husband asked her about what we were doing before 2pm. He said that something happened to him and he felt like a new person. That was a great confirmation confirming that what we did during my surrogate session had a profound effect on him. My colleague sent us her heartfelt gratitude for giving her husband a new life and for the gift she received of having an abundance of joy in her new relationship with her husband as she had always wanted.

Furthermore, I need to mention that my husband once was a true skeptic. He always told me that his mom taught him not to believe in anything. His upbringing had influenced him to be skeptical about many things including the work that I do. He did not believe in it. Back then, he said to me, *"I do not know what you do, and I don't even understand it, but I believe in you, if you believe in it, I'm ok with it. I don't have to believe or understand it."*

After he has gone through it with me, experiencing my success in helping people, witnessing so many miracles time after time, he finally opened himself up to it. A couple of years ago, he genuinely said to me, *"Patti, you are the only person on Earth that I believe in. How can I not believe?"* He does believe in the work that I do now, but he still doesn't understand it and I am okay with that. He is now my biggest fan. He became like our daughter now, in that he wants people to come to talk to me, to receive help. I had to remind him that I can't just impose my help on anyone. I'm not the one that will be doing the work; the desire has to come from the people who want to be helped. Otherwise, it will not work.

My husband and I took a cruise trip with my childhood friend this past summer. My friend and I have been friends for more than 40 years. She still lives in Thailand and I live here in the US, but our friendship is still blooming,

140

thanks to the advanced technology we have nowadays. When I heard that she was going to be in Miami for a conference, I organized a trip for us and included the people from Thailand who were attending this conference with her as well. There were 11 of us all together. We became acquainted with one another very quickly. While I was sitting alone looking at the vast ocean meditating, my husband had a friendly conversation with the group, and I realized afterwards that he talked about me proudly the whole time.

He suggested to them to approach me and just start talking with me about anything. He told them that they should take advantage of having the opportunity to talk with me, asking for guidance about life. He added that people travel from far away to come see me for a session and to receive guidance. Those people have to book their appointments 2 to 3 months in advance. He also wanted them to know how he has personally seen and heard how many lives have changed for the best. He enthusiastically encouraged them to take advantage of this golden opportunity and they did.

My cruise trip turned out to be a spiritual hang out. We had a group gathering every day, and one-on-one discussions in between. I helped them understand the power of the mind and the power of beliefs. I engaged them in hearing themselves talk so they could acknowledge their own thought processes and become aware of the thought processes within their minds that needed to be changed.

I helped them see every situation from two different perspectives, one from the perception of light and another from the perception of darkness. This was an effective way to engage them to acknowledge what needed to be changed and how they can make changes utilizing freewill and what they could change it to be. This is an extremely effective way to bring self-awareness and self-acknowledgement so that one can work on self-empowerment successfully.

Toward the end of the trip, I could tell that many of them became more enlightened and two of them who are already more advanced spiritually got the most out of it. This was very gratifying for me to have an opportunity to be of service to these people who live eleven-thousand miles away from me. They value their relationships with their loved ones more and know how to love and show love to their family and friends more naturally.

They are more productive as a result of having a new attitude toward their work with more passion to help them flow, glow and grow. They have become team players and know how to give support to all who they are involved with. Less competition, more cooperation! I utterly believe that the universe always provides what we need when we are ready. I understand how the synchronicity works better and better as I get to experience more of it. (Synchronicity means Source is in action anonymously.)

We keep in touch through our group chat and it is so nice to know that they are able to keep their own light bright and shine it out to others. Most importantly, it is a good and satisfying feeling to learn about my husband's approach toward those people expressing his belief in my work which I otherwise would not have known about. This demonstrates that we cannot change anyone, but we can always change ourselves and allow the positive changes to bring the good out in others.

I've been working on the changes in me and it has been affecting people around me, especially my husband who at one point was not on board with it. Now I've turned him into a believer. He has been making lots of good changes in his own life. He is more pleasant to be with and more in the flow with me. It makes it a lot easier for me to be me and carry on my work in being of service to people with genuine support from him.

By the way, he still doesn't know and doesn't understand how it works, but all is well. Maybe he will read this book one day and his mind will learn what his heart already knows.

I've been focusing on my self-acknowledgement. Even though sometimes I come across obstacles that others have created, I accept others for who they are and where they are in their level of consciousness. Within the 7.8 billion human souls on earth, there are only 4 types of souls:
(1) evolved and spiritual souls, (2) not evolved and not spiritual souls, (3) evolved but not spiritual souls and (4) spiritual but not evolved souls.

	Evolved	Not Evolved
Spiritual	1	4
Not Spiritual	3	2

The evolved and spiritual souls have the innerstanding of the creation of the universe, and the knowledge and tools to help them navigate through life with ease and flow. They are naturally loving, compassionate and kind, but if they forget what they know, they are not able to apply their wisdom, and can go out of harmony and become imbalanced. They may need to be reminded by the ones who are not evolved nor spiritual to keep being compassionate, practice non- judgement, stay harmonized and other lessons described earlier.

You will notice here that the ones who are not evolved and not spiritual are the greatest teachers of all because they will challenge the ones who are evolved and spiritual that are out of balance at their core. They will be triggered to go within so they can practice forgiveness and compassion and unconditional love without judgement toward them.

In order to evolve, we must master five crafts: (1) unconditional love, (2) compassion, (3) acceptance, (4) forgiveness and (5) trust. There is only one principle within the five crafts to mastery and that is non-judgement. We achieve mastery of all these crafts from practicing non-judgement. The non-evolved and non-spiritual souls are the best teachers. They exist to teach the evolved and spiritual souls to practice non-judgement so they can achieve mastery of those crafts.

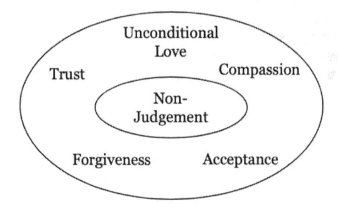

The ones who are evolved but not spiritual yet seem to pair up with the ones who are spiritual but not evolved. They aid each other by teaching and learning from one another so they can be more evolved and more spiritual together. The nature of the ones who are evolved but not spiritual are already at peace, in harmony, kind and loving. They easily accept others and have great compassion for other people. They may not have the spiritual understanding, but already put it into a daily spiritual practice without realizing it.

On the other hand, the ones who are spiritual but not evolved are the opposite. They have the knowledge, but they do not apply it. They forget to practice what they preach. They tend to give more of themselves to others and forget to take care of their own needs. They always want to help people. They do not realize that that helping others, but at the same time excluding, or ignoring their own needs, creates a deficit within them and limits what they have left to give. If they have fears, their fear can be passed on to others and contaminate them so-to speak. They could be helping others based on fear and that would not be good.

On the contrary, if their needs are fulfilled their help will be much more effective when delivered with pure love and compassion. Love gives light and wherever there is light there is no darkness. Imagine that! People tend to be either selfish or selfless, but there is something in between that we can practice being, a different self and that is **selfness**. Selfness is about being attentive to all that is required to find contentment. When we are selfness; we focus on working on ourselves to meet our needs to become wholesome, we will have 100 percent to give to others, not just what is left of us. This way we can be of service to others more effectively and successfully.

Again, the souls who are not evolved nor spiritual yet are the greatest teachers. They are being of service to others by giving people the opportunity to love them regardless and practice forgiveness that will help end their karma. It doesn't matter where we are in, regards to the soul levels of learning, we exist to be of service to one another, and to help each other wake up to a higher vision and to ascend.

I would like to go back now to talk some more about the power of the mind and to add two more stories to demonstrate it. This next story is from a recent session I had with a young client in his early 20's. He came in for a QHHT session to seek help resolving his issue with Lyme Disease. We always start a session with a pre-talk/an interview. During the interview, I helped him learn about the power of his mind and the power of belief and engaged him to claim the power of the Divine Light that lies within him. Then we carried on to the second step, the hypnosis. (I will explain more fully about the Divine power within us in the next chapter.)

During hypnosis, I requested healing for the Lyme disease and received guidance for the questions that he wanted to address to the Higher Self. His Higher Self gave the answers to all of his questions beyond his wildest expectations and told us that he had already completely eliminated the disease with the power of his mind before hypnosis. We were absolutely amazed and extremely happy!

He shared this information with his mother when he went back home. His mother was also my client and was the person that encouraged him to come see me for a session. Even though she already had her session with me and is a believer that anything is possible, she was still astonished by his news. This was again, truly a validation for her of just how powerful the mind is. She called me to set up another QHHT session with me and wanted to have a similarly phenomenal effect as the one her son experienced because she felt like she still had unfinished business in her heart.

She learned more about herself after coming to see me again. She mentioned that her ego sometimes got in her way, and that her belief system from her ego side may be interfering with her decision making, which made her heart feel heavy. During her first session with me, she was a harder nut to crack.

In her second session she was inspired by her son, and she was ready to allow herself to claim her divine power without any doubt.

She was ready to make all the necessary changes, surrendered to her truth and allowed peace and joy to come into her life. It turned out to be a beautiful gift to her entire family. She is the center of the circle of her family, so when she became more balanced it created a ripple effect on the rest of the people in her circle. The chain of a healthy mind continues through every connection with all the relationships that we have with others.

Her story also demonstrated that we are what we believe and that it is the power of the mind that sets our beliefs. At first, she was not willing or ready to give up her way of being to make the necessary changes. That's why her first session could only become as successful as she allowed it to be and as much as she believed that it would be. Then after her son demonstrated the change in himself, which instantaneously resulted in his self-healing, she was inspired to do more work within herself. She came in to see me for the second time already believing that it could be done. The manifestation already started taking place because she was ready and willing to surrender to her truth and her truth set her free. Our minds are that powerful! Our minds have the power to free us from the prisons we create within our own lives.

I have a personal self-healing story that my daughter suggested I share with the readers of this book. It was several years ago when I witnessed some of healing of some of my clients' eyesight after QHHT sessions. This phenomenon happened sometimes when my clients requested the healing of their eyesight. I believe it was because they had a strong desire and pure intention to resolve their eyesight and already believed that it could be done. It inspired me to request my own healing for my eyesight when I had my own surrogate session with Sue. I was hoping to have an instantaneous healing like some of my clients, but instead the Higher Self, suggested for me to practice self-healing and believe that it could be done.

I was given guidance on how to do it and the guidance was for me to try to wear my prescription eyeglasses less often, only when I needed them. I started reading with one eye at a time by covering an eye with my hand and tried to read solely with the other eye. I remember it was quite blurry at first, but as I allowed my eye to adjust itself gradually, I was able to see the words better little by little each time. Then when that eye seemed tired, I switched it to the other eye, following the same step. This practice was to train the eyesight back to the original. Afterwards, the guidance was to cover my three eyes (physical eyes and the third eye) with both hands and say this to myself, "My physical eyes can see as well as my third eye."

I took it to heart and practiced it daily. Gradually, my eyesight kept getting better and better. Months later I no longer needed to wear my glasses. My issues of being far sighted, near sighted and having astigmatism were no longer present. When I had my driver license renewed, I was told that I have perfect eyesight. I am no longer required to wear prescription glasses full-time while driving as listed in my previous license instructions. I feel so free as a result of liberating myself of the need to wear glasses. I asked the Higher Self if this is something that anyone could do and the 'they' said, (yes) "EVERYONE!" I would like to take this opportunity to share this valuable information with you here. It is a blessing indeed to know this.

There is one more story about my eyes that I would also like to mention here. I asked the Higher Self at a separate time about dry eyes issue. 'They' told me that it was because there was not enough oxygen in my system and that caused dryness in the body (skin, scalp, eyes, etc.) The guidance was for me to start exercising regularly to train the heart and lungs to pump blood more efficiently, allowing more oxygen to get to muscles and organs. I did just that and I no longer have dry eyes. Exercise has become a part of my daily routine ever since. This is something simple that we can do to help ourselves. It is simple, but highly effective. We have nothing to lose and much to gain, by taking these simple steps, right? Enjoy!

I hope these few stories I shared with you and that I personally experienced inspire you and let you find your inner knowing within your own truth. We need to find the real issue, the root cause, and uproot it. I have found that almost one hundred percent of the time, the beliefs embedded in the thought process involved will be found to be the main cause of the issue. To break away from the belief systems that do not benefit us, we need to raise our awareness so we can pay more attention to our thoughts. This way we can save ourselves from agony before it causes an illness or if the illness occurs, we can learn how to utilize the power within to help us to self-heal.

I feel the need to give the reminder again that our thoughts become words, words become actions, actions become our character and we are what we believe. If a belief creates disharmony and we keep dwelling on it and keep accumulating it, eventually we become dysfunctional and it will definitely affect our well-being. This is when the physical manifestation shows up to let us know that we are out of alignment and something must be done. Medicine can only work as a band-aid. Medicine can suppress the condition for a long while, but if we keep thinking the same thoughts, talking the same talk, acting the same actions, maintaining the same character and holding on to the same belief system, the dis-ease will continue to grow.

Imagine that we can take care of the dis-ease at its root and nurture it back to ease in peace and harmony before it manifests. We have a permanent solution and this reality is available for anyone who seeks and is willing to do the self-work and make some changes in their thinking and hold a different belief system that creates peace and joy.

It is best to have an awareness of what could happen before it happens. We only have to pay attention to our thoughts and become more aware of the power of the mind and the power of our belief systems. Once we are able to make changes, we will experience a major shift within ourselves in a profound way. We can heal ourselves and get to live our lives with a different perspective. The more refined that the perspective is, the more joy we will bring to everyone. Give this gift to yourself and let's pay it forward to others. Utilize the power of your mind with a healthy mindset and make sure that your belief system is in alignment with you, that it will support you and complement you throughout your life.

Check into your own belief system periodically to see which beliefs are not serving you well. Start making changes by utilizing your powerful mind to create the positive changes in your belief system which you desire. Watch how your life gets better and better every day in every way. Look inward and ask yourself if the belief system is yours or if it belongs to someone else and that you have bought into it. Freewill is your divine right. You can make as many changes as you wish. If anything has not been working well in your life, because there is stagnation occurring you can reassess things and correct your course.

Practice daily meditation to help you raise your awareness. Use meditation as one of your spiritual tools. It will be one of the most important tools that you have. It will give you the ability to identify what needs to be changed, so that you can make the changes that you need as you raise your conscious awareness of your thoughts. It is simple and if you make it your new good habit, and make this good new habit your priority, your life will be as joyful as you allow it to be. I've learned through my journey how important practicing a daily meditation is. It helps raise my awareness. That enables me to catch my thoughts as they are created and enhances my ability to discern between negative and positive thoughts, so I can utilize my freewill to eliminate old thought processes and old belief systems that do not serve me well.

Catch your thoughts, have discernment and choose whether you want to keep, modify or eliminate them within 3 seconds using the power of the mind. The self-work of staying connected is important. Now that I have done my self-work with meditation and understand the power of the mind, and utilize it, I am able to reconnect and stay connected with Divine Source in a profound way. I would like to share with you the amazing story of how I started making the connection with Divine Source in the next chapter.

Chapter Five:
The Higher Vision
of Patti's Connection with
Divine Source

My journey with Higher Vision started an awesome relationship for me with Source in ways that I could not and would not have predicted. The whole thing started with my illness 25 years ago and it woke me up from a deep sleep. I felt the need to find a way to not only stay alive, but also thrive through it. I was intrigued by everything that the Higher Vision had to offer. I was enjoying the process of taking the path to get to my destiny. There were many paths and many steppingstones that I experienced. Each one of them had one thing in common. They operate from within!

The universe will always provide us with what we need, but first we have to get ourselves ready to receive. Because of my illness, I was ready to open myself to anything that could help me to heal. When I decided to go back to practicing meditation, I realized that there was something about the practice that created peace and harmony in me. Obviously, it helped stabilize my condition during my hospital stay.

As I was searching for a more advanced method of meditation, I came across

Acupuncture and Chinese Herbs. It helped to balance my meridians and to cleanse toxins in my system. In the meantime, I learned Silva Mind and Body Connection. At the time I was not aware that I was learning how to do self-hypnosis.

I came to the conclusion as my awareness rose that meditation and hypnosis are operating at the same level of consciousness. It is the Alpha level, the first altered state of consciousness, the bridge to reconnect and stay connected with the wisdom of the Higher Self. When I was invited to learn Dharmakaya Vipassana Meditation (DVM) with the group, I was preconditioned to be able to relax easily, deeply and naturally. That definitely helped me to have an excellent outcome right away. This is why P'Somchai, my DVM teacher graciously offered to teach me all he knew, and it was very satisfying to both of us that I could embrace it with grace.

This was the time that my relationship with Source started, although I was not aware of it yet. Learning and practicing DVM was one of the highlights of my experience because I serendipitously learned how to regress into and connect to my past lives without initially realizing it. I realized that one of my past lives correlated with my liver illness. My liver completely healed instantly once I acknowledged, accepted and learned from the past life related to it.

Miraculously, the self-healing occurred after I accepted the outcome and worked on forgiveness of myself and others. Over a decade later, it seemed to me like the universe engaged me into taking this amazing journey and I am forever grateful for the opportunity to help so many people along with their own. If I did not have my own miraculous experience, I probably would not have had the interest to walk this path. My illness truly turned out to be a blessing indeed.

In order to help make it flow in this chapter regarding my relationship with Divine Source, I feel the need to briefly summarize my journey from Chapter Two. It will demonstrate how the universe synchronizes events for me to experience, to learn and to grow from all of them.

During the time that I was progressing with learning DVM, Dr. Hu helped me with Acupuncture and herbs. She also introduced Qigong into my life. I was able to embrace my experiences with DVM and Dr. Hu. Shortly after, Reiki was introduced to me unexpectedly. I loved it so much that I became a Reiki Master.

The life force of source energy is the same within Qigong and Reiki, but the technique to harness the life force is totally different. I came to the conclusion that even the Pure Bioenergy technique I had an opportunity to learn a few years ago also accesses energy from the same source. I completely respect the different approaches to accessing and working with energy. Each of the techniques has a unique way of focusing energy, although I am certain they all access the exact same energy. All is well, as it always will be. As long as they work, I'm all in with various techniques. I was able to apply my knowledge from all the modalities to help people with healing and have had phenomenal success.

It is exciting to learn and be able to utilize this Source energy to help people. It turned out that I had to heal myself before embarking on my journey to support others in their own healing process. It reminded me of the day when I had a post meditation discussion with our group. I excitedly shared with my Guru my new discovery with healing energy that I had recently cultivated. I told him about my strong desire to help people with it. The monk acknowledged my pure intention but discouraged me from focusing on it. His explanation made sense to me, I needed to focus on dealing with my own karma first, before I could deal with other-people's karma. After that conversation with him, I decided to focus on meeting my needs first and it was exactly what needed to be done at the time and I'm glad that I listened. Forgiveness is the best and magical way to end karma because it closes the karmic account that we may have with self or with others.

Consequently, I stayed focused on my growth by reading more books, taking more workshops, going to various conferences, and of course, practicing daily meditation. One of the books I came across was "Many Lives, Many Masters[4]". This book was written by the well-known author, Brian Weiss, MD., who is a Psychiatrist who became famous after publishing this book. He has written many books, and yes, I read them all.

Many Lives, Many Masters was written in 1988 and it is still one of the most popular books in this genre. The story is about how Dr. Weiss was trying to help his patient through the traditional regression hypnosis practice that he knew which was to help regress his patient back to a very young age. His patient could not remember any traumas before she was 3 years of age and he wanted to see if he could find more information before that time to see if there were any unusual circumstances that could explain her unexplainable behaviors.

Unexpectedly, he took her back multiple lifetimes and he was extremely surprised by his findings. He was able to help her a lot more than he could have initially, due to the past life regression type of hypnotherapy he stumbled

---

[4] Weiss, B. (1988). *Many Lives, Many Masters: The True Story of a Prominent Psychiatrist, His Young Patient, and the Past-Life Therapy That Changed Both Their Lives.* Simon & Schuster, Inc.: New York.

upon. This was a trigger point for me to want to take on my next endeavor. I found a local teacher in my hometown. I took training and became a Certified Hypnotherapist, a Past Life Regressionist.

I had successful sessions with people bringing in information from their past lives with the technique, but I was not sure how I could help them with the healing from the way I received it from my own regression during my meditation practice. I believed that there must have been more to healing past life trauma and sure enough, I'm forever grateful that there was. This is when I came across one of Dolores Canon's books, *"The Three Waves of Volunteers and The New Earth[5]."*

I became intrigued and inspired by her work. I attended her lectures about this book twice, once in Front Royal, VA and the second time in Andover, MA. Dolores asked me later on during our personal training in Arkansas, *"Why did you attend the same lecture of mine twice?"* I replied to her that I couldn't get enough of her. I was captivated by everything about her work and couldn't wait to sign up for her Level 1 class and lucky for me shortly after that there was one available in Andover, MA.

---

[5] Cannon, D. (2011). *The Three Waves of Volunteers and The New Earth*. Ozark Mountain Publishing: Huntsville.

This was the time that I had the opportunity to attend her lecture for the second time. This was an amazing opportunity for me to learn from the great master. Not only did the learning of her method spark my relationship with Source, it gave me the opportunity to help other people make the same connection as well. Since I was already a Certified Hypnotherapist by IMDHA (International Medical and Dental Hypnosis Association), I understood most of the basic foundation, and ultimately, I advanced beyond what I can easily describe in words.

I arranged for one of my classmates to meet up with me in my hotel room to exchange sessions with one another so we could immediately practice QHHT together. Because I was already familiar with the process, I was able to help support her session on me with ease. We had great success and I had the opportunity to share our results in front of the classroom the next day. In retrospect, I remember walking down to the hotel lobby that night to buy some bottled water and I came across another classmate who was quite eccentric. He asked me to practice QHHT on him.

Of course, I took the opportunity and I am glad I did. His session was literally out of this world. I do not remember the details since it was a while back, although I do remember the feeling of excitement that I experienced from conducting his session because it was so convoluted. I enjoyed sharing the experience in class the next morning. The session was a bizarre experience, but it did not scare me at all.

Consequently, I became hooked and very intrigued with Quantum Healing work even more. An experience that was unexplainable to me occurred during that weekend. It started with me suffering from a Urinary Tract Infection (UTI) the first day of traveling, which was bad timing due to its possible effect the outcome of my training experience. There was nothing I could do but just ride it out. For some reason, it magically disappeared by itself just being a part of everything as I sat in the classroom with others. I believe it was the beautiful energy that we all brought to the group, because others mentioned the same thing with similar stories of how some of their symptoms were also healed just from being there.

I had an amazing time and I loved every moment of it. I travelled back home on cloud nine and did not want that feeling to end. I am glad it didn't. I arrived at the airport and my husband was nowhere in sight to pick me up. I called him wondering about where he could be. He said he was home and forgot that he had to pick me up from the airport. I could tell from his tone of voice that he did not forget, rather that he sounded mad and perhaps just wanted to take it out on me that way. I was too happy to react back negatively. I pretended that I did not know that he was playing with me. I just joyfully told him that, *"It is okay. I am already at the airport, and I will just sit here, and meditate until you can come."* That is exactly what I did.

I do not remember how long I was sitting there because as I said earlier, I was on cloud nine and did not care about anything else, but just staying at that frequency. When he arrived, I remembered how agitated he was, and it convinced me even more that he did not forget. It was his way of showing to me that he did not appreciate that I took the trip. Again, I was way too happy to react back at him. I was still upbeat with the excitement and could not wait to share my experience with him. He did not understand any of it. My joyful energy was a saving grace he could not resist, and it saved the situation.

That incident and his behavior demonstrated how much he was against the direction I was taking. I had no idea until experiencing his behavior, because he never said anything prior to that. My husband was a hard nut to crack. He had a hard time understanding this part of me, but I never let him affect what I chose to believe or what journey I wanted to take. Later on, as he had a variety of experiences with me that were quite favorable, the wall he constructed began to come down a little bit at a time. He began to change his tone. He told me that it was okay. He didn't have to understand or know what I was doing. He told me he believed in me and knows I believe in what I am doing. I just let him be himself and knew he would give me the support that I needed, even if he didn't believe in it himself.

Time passed and he could not keep his wall up anymore because he witnessed so many phenomenal outcomes and he could not be in denial any longer. Afterward I became one of the Dolores's recommended practitioners under her new program 10 months before she passed away. As a result, I became busier and busier. Word of mouth started to spread, and I started booking clients for QHHT sessions and soul coaching for months in advance. Clients travelled from all over the country and even other countries to come to see me for their sessions. We had amazing outcomes.

I realized he was starting to change his view, his belief about my work when he asked me this, *"Did you know then how well you would be doing with this work? Looking back on your life, did you realize when you started that you would be this successful with it?"* I quickly replied, *"Nope, it did not enter into my mind at all, but I totally believed in it and wanted to pursue it hoping to help people."* Then weeks later, he added, *"Patti you are the only person on earth that I believe in. How can I not believe when I get to see and be a part of this journey with you now?*" This was very inspiring for me and supports me to keep going and to help as many people as I can and as I was trained to do by the great master with her brilliant method.

My husband is now in the flow, giving me all the support that I need, but still doesn't understand it. Back when I started, I had no idea where my work would take me. I only listened to my heart and it felt right! He is now my biggest fan and has started talking about me to other people in a positive way mentioning that he doesn't even understand what I really do or how it works, although he is convinced that it does work, based on the transformations he has seen time and time again. The biggest proof of all was his own experience with the emotional healing from the result of a surrogate session that Sue and I did for him with the help of the Higher Self. He can no longer be in denial nor resists the flow.

Furthermore, it was to my enormous surprise that he suggested to some new friends that we meet during our vacation that they take advantage of the opportunity to get guidance from me while we were together. As a result of this I was able to recognize my husband's hidden admiration for me, that otherwise I would not have known if those new friends hadn't told me about it. It was genuine and I am honored for his change of heart in regard to

166

my work, which he previously admitted to me he did not believe in, nor think would work.

Through the changes I have witnessed in my very own inner circle, I have gained even more trust in the universe and utterly believe that all of us are a part of the One. We all have the same opportunity to create anything we wish with the energy within us. I work on myself daily making sure that I stay connected with the Divine Source that led me to find the ultimate truth and connecting me to the Source within me. This is the same Source that is always there inside all of us, waiting patiently for us to reconnect and stay fully connected. It is very loving and always has our back and our best interests in mind.

Since I have made this connection, I will never let it go. It is the ultimate relationship that One can have. I wish this experience for everyone on earth. It is the unconditional love essence that naturally is part of us at a spiritual or energetic level. All it takes is to open up and allow us to receive it. Make it simple! Simplicity is the key to unlocking all potentials. It is easier and simpler to swim with the current rather than against it. Make the connection with the Source of Divine love within and let it overflow to others naturally and this is so. Once we make that connection we never run out of love. Love is always flowing through the heart unconditionally.

My deep connection happened when I received Dolores' invitation to take part in her pilot training to become one of her recommended practitioners. I was nervous and decided to try to prepare myself for the trip. I did an unthinkable thing. I hypnotized my friend, Sue, as me, hoping to tap into my Higher Self through her. Yes, I hit a jackpot! Not only did I tap into my higher self, I connected to the ultimate Higher Self (Oneness of all).

As I was playing around with my new endeavor, I realized that I tapped into the Source of knowledge and worked with the Oneness of Divine Source consciousness, the infinite. (Whatever we want to call this energy. To me all the names seem to fit in their own way.) Meaning that all becomes one at that level of consciousness— where Source, Sue and I tapped into the Akashic record of the person we were focusing on, which happened to be my record that day. The Akashic record is like an enormous photographic film of all the experiences of our planet and the people in it. It was a brand-new experience that I did not quite understand the potential of well enough until much later on.

I became dedicated to having my own sessions with Sue as my surrogate. I enjoy having conversation with Source through her because her consciousness stays completely out of the way. The experiences I have had have been very credible to me and have gained my trust of the information I receive that I know in my heart that it comes from a Source of purity. The universe has set it up so that Sue and I have our regular visit every couple of months and I always ask her to let me gain insight by doing a surrogate session for me during every visit.

I was totally surprised during one of our sessions when Source asked me to help my husband. I was not sure how it could help and was wondering what Source meant by that because I tried to put him under hypnosis three times without the kind of success that we should have had. I decided to do a surrogate session for my husband with Sue's help and it worked magically. I realized the potential of being able to help more people by having Sue serve as the surrogate subject for others as needed, and thankfully, Sue graciously accepted to team up with me to help others with this new tool.

I felt so loved and cared for by Source, therefore, I learned to trust even more. I always asked for a final message for me from Source and for a long while, they gave me this, *"Keep soaring"*, and after that, *"Keep trusting"*, and *"Keep shining your light"* and lately, *"Keep writing."* Yes, I will always listen to the guidance with gratitude and yes, I'm writing!

I enjoy receiving new guidance from Source and I trust the process and the information that is always filled with enormous love and light. I feel that Source always has everyone's best interests in mind and will give us what we need, but not always what we want. Source makes things so simple and when we stop complicating things, we can really enjoy living life with simple abundance. An abundance of love, peace, joy, harmony, good relationships, gratitude are always available to us. All is available within and waiting to be claimed. I dedicate this entire book to this matter, and I will show you the simplest way to bring it out from within in Chapter 6, The Higher Vision of Divine Source. It will be the highlight of this book and why this book was written.

Source has been wanting me to write this book and it took me years to trust that I could. English is my second language and I was not sure about what to write. Also, my lovely daughter teased me a few times, she said, *"Mom, you write so Asian!"* I used to laugh at her comment and felt the need to write less Asian. I realized my sentence structure tended to be based on how I translated my Thai thoughts into English writing, and it sounded Asian to her. Over time I became more aware and able to write more effectively.

As I keep progressing consciously, I realized that it is my unique way of expression.

I am bilingual (actually, one of my clients pointed out to me that I am trilingual because she said I speak Thai, English and Vibration language, and yes, I can see that now). It is my way of keeping balance among my Eastern, Western and Cosmic ways of Being. I started to appreciate my way of being different and feel comfortable with it more and more. I now know by being different I can make a difference in the world.

I am also naturally ambidextrous. I was trained to use my right hand from a very young age even though I am a lefty. My grandmother, who raised me since birth kept telling me, *"Dear, eat with your right hand. Your left hand is for wiping your butt only."* This memory of grandma makes me giggle every time I think about her. So, I learned to use my right hand to eat and to write to please grandma, but I feel most comfortable using my left hand to do anything else. I was wondering just recently, if I could write with my left hand, so when I did try it, I realized that I really could. I have been slowly discovering the various things I can do if I try. By saying this, I feel very comfortable to bring in the balance of energy of my wholeness and just flow with it. It has helped me gain more confidence that I did not have at an earlier time.

I had an experience that really encouraged me to start writing. It was in 2013 when I attended a psychic medium gathering event. There were a few hundred participants in the room, and they were hoping to be called by the spirits of their loved ones through the help of the famous psychic twins, Allyson and Adele. The twins have been famous for their authenticity and ability to serve as mediums who make a connection for the living with their loved ones on the other side of the veil. I'd seen them on TV and appreciated their natural ability to serve humanity with their gifts. I attended the gathering many times and had witnessed the connection that the twins made for one of my friends as well, and it brought tears to her eyes.

In one of the events, they called on me, but I didn't respond because I was not aware it was for me. They mentioned something about The Grand Prix event, located near the Inner Harbor in Baltimore. I then remembered my husband was at The Grand Prix event. He was working at one of the hotels there during the event. The roads were closed down to set up for the Grand Prix Rally, so nobody could go in or out. All the workers and spectators had to park their cars outside the starting location and my husband decided to just hang out afterwards and watch the race.

Since I was not at the event, I was not sure the comment was for me, so I did not reply at first. The twin sisters kept asking if anyone had been there, because there was a message for someone, and they needed someone in the audience who perhaps was connected with this event. Nobody claimed it and they said, *"No one? Nobody was there?"* I slowly raised my hand and said, *"I was not there, but my husband was."* Since, I was the only person who even knew anything about the event, the twin said, **"It is for you then! Your guides are here, and they wanted to give you this message - Get going on your writing!"** I had goose bumps down my spine receiving this message which was so on point. I knew I'd been avoiding it because of the lack of confidence I felt. I was still learning and growing spiritually and did not feel I was ready to claim my light at the time.

It turned out that the message the sisters provided me with triggered a sense of urgency to begin writing. I felt the need to at least give it a try. There was a full audience participating in this event, but I was the one to receive this message and I wanted to honor that. I started writing just after that event, but I succeeded in writing with only one chapter, then I put it away. I remember asking Source about what 'they' wanted me to write and what the name of the book would be.

Source said to write about my journey and how I started to walk this path and all of the learning that has resulted from my life experiences that brought me to where I am. At that time, I believe I was not fully in the correct flow with myself. I was still in the midst of soul searching. I did not feel like I had enough to share so I left it alone until months ago. Then I had an urge to write and felt motivated to do so. Once I was committed, my body just started waking up earlier than usual. I got to work on my writing, before I knew it, I realized that I had prepared a draft of the entire book without recognizing it.

The summer of 2018, I received an invitation to host my own talk show and I consulted with Source about it, if it was something that I should pursue. 'They' (Source) gave me the guidance to go for it and also gave me the name for the show, *"**Get It Straight from The Source**"*, which I found brilliant. After a brief training at Bold Brave Media Studio, I was ready to launch my own Radio Talk Show. It became another steppingstone toward my writing, but I was not aware of it at the time.

I believe it was the part of me, that sometimes could be a perfectionist. It pushed me to invest the time to prepare a script for the one hour I committed to do the show each week. I revised, revised and revised some more until I was satisfied. I asked some of my friends to edit my scripts for the talks. I hosted the show every week for six months. For some shows I invited my clients as guests to share their phenomenal sessions with the audience. I enjoyed it at the time, but after six months, the passion was not there anymore because the preparation was so intense that I just didn't feel like I wanted to keep up with it.

When I was ready to write, I realized after I pulled up the typed talks which I had created for my radio show would serve as content for my book. I would do a little writing in the morning when I woke up with an inspirational thought or a keyword on a subject which gave me the motivation to add it to my writing. I realized how much joy I experienced doing this writing for Source. Source said, *"Keep writing. We want you to write, so we give you all the support that you need. Just keep writing."* By the way, I need to mention that the conversation between Source and I happened regularly during my own surrogate sessions with Sue.

As I mentioned, I became dedicated to my own sessions, so every chance I had, I asked Sue to be my surrogate subject. She is so kind to let me hypnotize her as me and allow me to receive more guidance from Source. I'm a very curious person, so, I never run out of questions that I wish to address to Source and 'they' are so kind and loving that 'they' never get tired of answering me. I came across this process of connecting with Divine Source in 2012. I was nervous about receiving intensive personal training directly from Dolores and felt the need to prepare myself to meet with her and be at my best. It turned out that it has become my new normal to have a continuous connection with Source ever since. The synchronicity of all things is so divine, and we just have to trust it and be in the flow with it. Again, thoughts become words, words become actions, actions become our character and we are what we believe. Anything is possible. What we believe we become, and the universe is always ready to engage in partnership with us provide help in a synchronistic way. All is well.

I've learned so much about myself and from knowing that as long as I stay in alignment with Source all will be well. Just keeping my vibration high and focused on light, love, peace, joy and harmony, and not swinging into fear, I am able to serve as a conduit as a vibration-ship to others that I work with.

The confidence keeps growing because I trust that I am not the one that will do the work. It is between the people and Source. The universe and I will always give our all, but the work is not one hundred percent automatic because we still have to deal with people's freewill; the will to accept and to receive. I focus on helping everyone that I work with to find their truth that lies within them and help them claim it with the help of scientific facts and also from the downloads I receive from the universe.

Although, I receive the same concept and the same download for everyone, the information comes in at the frequency at the level of the receiving end, so the information is tailored to each person receiving it. Since I get to translate the frequency into words, I often giggle about some of the translations that are so brilliant and simple. I'm aware of how I wouldn't be able to come up with it on my own. As I hear myself talk, I get to expand myself with more and more knowledge from Source. I no longer feel the need to read as much or want to take workshops like I did before, because I really enjoy learning directly from Source. I wish to pass the wisdom on to everyone who seeks it.

I believe that just because we do not know that things exist, it doesn't mean that they do not exist. I still am in awe finding out more and more about many things from Source that exist whether from my own surrogate sessions, or from my clients' sessions, or even from the downloads that I've been receiving for others. It has opened me up to the infinite realm and it is comforting to have the awareness of the synchronicity and Divine reason behind everything. It encourages me to stay neutral and be in the flow with any circumstances, because Source shows me that in every situation there are two perspective to look from. One is the perspective of darkness and the other is the perspective of light. When we look at any situation from the perspective of darkness, right away we will see issues and problems. If we look at those issues and problems with a magnifying-glass based on fear, we will blow them up in our faces.

On the other hand, when we choose to look at the same situation from a perspective of light and not make what we are looking at a problem, there is no problem, but only an opportunity to grow. There is always something to learn from someone as we are co-existing and are here to be of service to one another. When we look for light, we see light. When we look for darkness, we see darkness Seek the light.

 There is a Native American parable about two wolves. One wolf is of the light (love) and one is of the darkness (fear). The wolf we feed is the one that becomes stronger and leads our lives.

There are two major reasons why we are here on earth, to evolve further and to be of service to mankind. We all have the same opportunity to experience life with the help of one another. We challenge each other to learn and grow in every circumstance so we can evolve back to LOVE, the unconditional love. When we are more evolved, we are more equipped to be of service to others more successfully and more effectively. Imagine that we are being of service to someone, we always want to give our all, but if our all is too limited, we will not be able to provide what is needed to be successful and effective. When our hearts are filled up with unconditional love, we are giving one hundred percent of all that we have. When we connect to and share unconditional love, we become portals of infinite energy. We have to become the essence of what we are giving.

In the next chapter I will talk about what I've learned from Source about being all and giving all. I've been using this concept to help so many people and it has changed many lives, including the people in their circles. As I follow that same teaching, I walk the talk and it has profoundly changed my life and the lives of the people who are a part of my circle. I'm ready to share the wonderful concepts I've received from Source with you in the following chapter.

It is my purest intention to pay it forward to all who are seeking a profound change in life and find the ultimate change from the teaching I received straight from Source. Weekly for six months I shared this message on the show "Get It Straight from the Source." I am sharing the essence of that message directly with you from the heart of source to your heart. This change will be a gift that we all can give to ourselves and everyone we know and love. In this following chapter, take your time reading it, and go back to the information that you resonate with as often as you need to. Contemplate on the meaning of the guidance and feeling which vibrates in your heart as you are accepting light, vibration, and frequency. This is the teaching that has helped so many people become more enlightened. Allow yourself to lighten up and brighten up with love and light while you are claiming your self-worth and ascend. Once you claim it, own it, embody it, it is yours forever, and it can never be taken away again if you do not give your power away.

Chapter Six:
The Higher Vision
of Divine Source

This subject is very dear to my heart and I have a strong desire to share this valuable information with you. I received it straight from the Source of knowledge through the work that I do, and it has been helping me so much with my growth. In my previous chapters I talked a lot about quantum healing work and shared some of my phenomenal experiences. I felt it was important to support and validate the information, so both your mind and heart would receive the message.

I feel the need to talk a little about the Soul Coaching work that I also do. I utilize my gift of clairaudience to help my clients receive emotional healing through self-discovery during our conversations. I let people know that "**I**" do not do the healing. I serve as a conduit to help people heal themselves by discovering their truth, and the truth will set them free. I mentioned earlier that I am intuitive. I hear frequency and interpret vibration. I translate it into feeling and vibrate it into image and language in the physical realm. I operate as an empath, as a vibration-ship to others that I work with. Ever since I claimed this gift, I have trusted it and allow it to be my essential tool in helping people bridge with their truth.

Soul Coaching sessions are a helpful tool to aid people with emotional healing, because emotional issues typically create dis-ease which often lead to disease in the physical form. Most importantly, it is essential for all of us to find our authentic self and make a shift of consciousness so we can be in alignment with the new energy during the process of an ascension.

Source told me this during one of my own sessions, **"Do not stop giving the downloads. Keep listening and let us work through you."** Not only do I really enjoy bringing the downloads to people and hear myself voice the information, I'm delighted to listen, learn and grow so much from it as well. Although, I bring in the same information based on the same concept for everyone, the frequency is uniquely different depending on the vibration of the person being supported. The frequency may be different, but the content contains the same meaning. The truth is still the same. I realized that this concept has helped thousands of souls to evolve and ascend with the process.

I offer this beautiful gift to you in this chapter. My intention is to help anyone who seeks to find themselves and be free; free to live life in joy and realize their highest potential as a soul in the physical realm. See if you can resonate with any of this information. If you do, I strongly suggest that you **claim it**, **own it** and **embody** it. It is our own self-worth that we may not be aware of and when we become aware, even the sky is no longer a limit. The ability to manifest abundance in your reality is at hand.

Many of my clients came to see me for sessions; feeling lost, hopeless, like their backs were against the wall. It seemed to them like they had already exhausted all available resources. When they came across Dolores's information, reading her books and watching her YouTube channel, they started to have hope. They became intrigued and inspired by her information and that quickly sparked their interest to look into the new alternative styles of healing. They started looking for someone who practices her modality. Thankfully I am one of her proteges and that has provided me the opportunity to represent her and help more people through the QHHT modality.

When I work with people, it is extremely important that I let them know that the ball is in their court. I'm not doing the work. It is between them and Source. I serve as a conduit, bridging between them and Source. It is my pleasure to help people find their truth, knowing that they have all the tools they need. I show them the options that they already have, but they may not be aware of. Then they can make the necessary changes in their lives with a great deal of understanding, certainty and confidence.

We need to find the main cause of their troubles and make the essential changes at the root level. The intellect and the wisdom must be integrated to make changes that promote the growth for this evolution (returning to love). This will be a permanent solution once we understand ourselves and know our powerful divine selves well. Philosophers say, *"Know thyself."* This is only a small part of the picture. I say to you, *"Know you are love and be one with your soul essence. You are much more than the self. The Higher Self is a part of you and one with Divine Source."*

Many of the people I get to help become enlightened at the end of our sessions. It may take an entire day for us to make it work, but it is worth all the effort. Especially, after they had exhausted all the options which they thought they had. You don't have to wait lifetimes to become conscious of your Higher Self. It happens instantly when you just allow it to happen. Seek and you will find! It is already a part of you within you.

I do receive updates from my clients periodically and it is to my delight to know that they are able to maintain that state of mind. It is certainly a life changing experience for everyone who is ready to make changes. I've been helping people with this same basic information that I received straight from Divine Source. My pure intention is to pay it forward to you here. Life will definitely become more pleasant and joyful once we find what we are looking for. We will not find it anywhere outside of us but only from within ourselves! I too, have learned more and more from this process as I've helped people find themselves with the same teaching from Source. People come from all walks of life feeling the need to find answers as they search for their truth.

The authentic truth is already there within us and waiting for us to discover it. Like I said earlier, I teach the same concept to everyone, but I download the information and translate it into words at the level of the person's frequency which is perfectly aligned with that person's level of consciousness. The life changing experiences that we get to listen to and learn from The Source of love, light and knowledge are more valuable than anything physical. It helps us with our soul evolution so we can grow spiritually. We get to do less but BE more. **Be the light that we are here to be so we can shine the light within us and see our finest self and spark that same light in others.**

This is the same light that we originated from. The most powerful, loving light that is so pure and always has our best interests in mind and will always honor our freewill as to how we wish to operate and experience life. This powerful loving light has no judgement. There is no good or bad, right or wrong. It is what it is, and it is what unconditional love is all about. Love is within us. We come from love. When we connect to Source, we feel the big love of the universe that is in us.

I would like to take this opportunity to inspire you now, so you can learn and gain knowledge about this truth. When we inspire, we take in light, then share it with others. I am sharing this light with you now. I'm sharing some of the most valuable knowledge I've learned from the Source of knowledge with you. Go ahead and explore the information that you resonate with and see what you can do to make it work for you.

It is priceless when you know what you need to know about the simplicity of a life that has great potential. It will help raise your awareness of who you truly are and who you are capable of being at your best. You can stop looking outside of yourself and just allow yourself to look deeply within and find your own divine power there waiting there to be discovered. It is my highest intention to gift you with this knowledge as a guiding light. I do believe that this light will guide you and give you support throughout your journey. Just allow yourself to tap into the wisdom from Divine Source within you and allow yourself to blossom into your finest self as you make the changes needed for your personal growth. Let your wisdom guide you through the exploration of your path with joy today.

First, I would like to build a basic foundation for us. It may be basic, but it is extremely essential. We need to build a strong foundation so we can build a stable structure on top of it. As you resonate with any of this information that I'm bringing to you, you will feel it within your heart. If you believe it to be your truth, make sure you allow yourself to open up your heart and your mind to accept it with love and gratitude; that knowledge will set you free. Allow yourself to explore it without judgement. Allow yourself to explore it from the perspective of light and that means there is no good or bad or even right or wrong. Just allow yourself to shift the paradigm to see the light Source offers to you and expand yourself with this light, and this is so.

We've been living our lives under deceptive programming and under other peoples' controlling belief systems long enough. The limitations of social standards, upbringing and our physical and social environments have led us to the experiences that have built us as we are and frequently broken us down. Whether we are built up by an experience or we are broken down by it depends on the foundational beliefs that we take on. The accumulation of living life under a single false belief or a system of thousands of beliefs can have a huge negative effect on our health and on our relationships with others.

False beliefs can cause us to have fears, hatred, anger, resentment, guilt, shame, and sadness. We unconsciously turn those emotions inward to sabotage ourselves emotionally and therefore create health issues without realizing it. The troubles always start from the same root cause and that cause is being judgmental toward ourselves and others. It doesn't matter whether we are being judgmental toward self or toward others. The results are the same because when we judge ourselves or judge someone else, we open ourselves up to react with the negative emotions which affect us deeply. When this becomes a habit, we accumulate the chain of negative feelings and beliefs.

Every thought that the heart accepts becomes an emotion and that emotion turns into a feeling. When we feel any emotion that is created from a negative thought, the body will react and release stress hormones, adrenaline, and cortisol[6]. These hormones destroy the healthy cells in the body and can lead to disease, depending on the vulnerability of a person's body and severity of the stress.

---

[6] Mayo Clinic Staff (2019). *Chronic Stress Puts Your Health at Risk.* Downloaded from https://www.mayoclinic.org/healthy-lifestyle/stress-management/in-depth/stress/art-20046037

This is how we make ourselves sick. The stress hormones are created as a reaction to negative emotion. Stress hormones are stored in the cellular memory and turn into emotional baggage. It does not happen overnight. The accumulation of these storage emotions may not be shown until the system is overloaded, and then presents itself in physical form.

If we are powerful enough to make ourselves sick, we can utilize the same power within us to make ourselves well. Stress is created by our perception of a situation and how we react to it. We can choose to live from a higher perspective and avoid storing emotional baggage. Imagine living life feelings of rage and fear. Just see how this can affect every relationship that you have with others. We tend to say things we do not mean when we are angry, and of course, we cannot take those words back after we feel better. Also, if we make any decision based on fear, it will definitely block us from moving forward and we may make choices that won't help us in the long run.

On the contrary, when we think good thoughts that our heart accepts, they turn into positive emotion, the body starts reacting and releases positive chemicals. These positive chemicals are dopamine, oxytocin, serotonin, and endorphins. They support the enhancement of cell rejuvenation, regeneration of healthy cells and restoring of the structures and systems of our bodies. This is how we can make ourselves well. Allow yourself to make some good changes with new belief systems that you can resonate with and allow yourself to claim your authentic truth and get good use of it. Be conscious of the thoughts that your heart accepts and be aware of your powerful ability to make changes to get yourself well.

Chemical	Associated Effect[7]
Dopamine	Good or bad habit forming
Oxytocin	Creates trust and a loving feeling
Serotonin	Feeling of accomplishment or recognition
Endorphins	Natural painkiller

We are a part of the same origin and this origin is the infinite energy of unconditional love. This infinite energy of unconditional love does not have a name, but let's come up with some kind of name so we can have something to refer to it by. How about divine being? Or how about God? God is love, the unconditional love that is infinite. How about Divine Source? The source that is the origin of everything. How about the Creator? The creator that creates everything. How about the Absolute,

[7] Kandler, M. (2019). *Four Brain Chemicals That Make You Happy.* Downloaded from https://www.happyfeed.co/research/4-brain-chemicals-make-you-happy

the Infinite, the All That Is, All Mighty, Supreme being, Over Soul, Divine energy, The Higher Self, Oneness, Love or Light? Well, any of these names seem to fit, right? Let's pick a name out of these options now. Let's call this infinite energy of unconditional love "The Divine Being". The Divine Being that is perfect, kind, and pure with unconditional love.

Sometimes our critical mind, the left brain blocks us from connecting to the invisible realm of love, the Higher Self and Divine Source (God). There are scientific explanations of how we are connected to Divine Being, that can support the mind to release itself and consciously connect with the heart. Gregg Braden studied the connection between the numerical representations of ancient languages, the periodic table of the elements and human DNA patterns.

One of his finding was that the top layer of human DNA has the message "God eternal within the body". He also describes in detail how the 4 main elements of DNA, hydrogen, nitrogen, oxygen and carbon relate to the letters Y-H-W-H. These are the consonants of the word Yahweh, the word for God found over 6.500 times in the old testament Christian bible. If you feel his research would help you consciously connect your heart and mind it would be worth reading. See the footnote below for reference[8].

Let's bring science further into this conversation for a little bit. I love and appreciate science because science has solid proof for many phenomena. Scientists want proof for everything, *"We believe it when we see it."* We want to move the mind beyond that to, *"We believe it, that's why we will see more of it."* In this sense believing is seeing, rather than seeing is believing. Just because we do not know something exists, does not mean it does not exist.

There are scientists that I appreciate greatly: Gregg Braden[9] (mentioned in the previous paragraph), Joe Dispenza[10] and Bruce Lipton[11]. They are three new age scientists that have introduced a new way of looking at things with descriptions of human evolution and their own experiences. I strongly encourage readers to check out their works and learn to expand their self-awareness further (see the footnotes for references to some of their writing).

---

[8] Braden, G. (2005). *The God Code: The Secret of our Past, the Promise of our Future.* Hay House Inc.: New York.

[9] Braden, G. (2019). *The Science of Self-Empowerment: Awakening the New Human Story.* Hay House Inc.: New York.

[10] Dispenza, J. (2019). *Becoming Supernatural: How Common People Are Doing the Uncommon.* Hay House Inc.: New York.

[11] Lipton, B. (2008). *Biology of Belief Unleashing the Power of Consciousness, Matter, and Miracles.* Hay House Inc.: New York.

I am in alignment with their new belief systems based on scientific evidence which support the wisdom that this book offers.

Let's explore it further now! Ever since Nikola Tesla came out with his statement that energy is everywhere, scientists wanted to have proof of that, and there now is proof. They have proved now that yes, energy is everywhere, and they call this energy "**neutrinos**". I didn't even know how to spell the word neutrino until a client who is a Physicist from New York taught me how to spell this word. She knows the conventional views of quantum physics by heart, although she believes there must be more to it.

She is a spiritual person and she told me that she took all the workshops that grabbed her attention and read all the spiritual books she could find; but does not feel complete or satisfied and that she is still in search of the complete truth. She found the completion that already lay within her during our QHHT session. I helped her realize that it was there within herself the entire time as I'm helping you now to realize the same wisdom. She felt complete and wholesome at the end of the session and it was gratifying for me to serve her in her journey.

When we started talking about the measurement of the energy in everything, she explained how physicists invented some kind of device that can measure energy everywhere. With that device, they tried to measure the neutrinos in the universe, but of course, they couldn't! The data showed them that the neutrinos in the universe are infinite and could not be quantified. They don't understand it and they don't understand God, so they named those neutrinos in the universe "the God particle". Then they measured the neutrinos in human beings, and found the exact same neutrinos, God particles within each one of us and numbered in the hundreds of trillions.

Science is now catching up with spirituality. The left brain (the critical thinking, problem solving part of us) is starting to be able to describe and innerstand what the right brain (our intuitive and creative side) already knows. We are a part of infinite Source, God particles. We carry the same exact energy. We may be tiny little divine sparks in comparison to the infinite source, but we are still extremely powerful holding hundreds of trillions of particles of Divine Source energy within us. It is the energy of unconditional love.

Yes, this is the proof that we have the same quantum energy of the god particle in us. That raised the question, **"Where is that energy in our bodies?"** Energy has no form and energy cannot be seen with the naked eye. Every organ in our bodies has some kind of form and can be seen. The heart, the lungs, the brain and everything in our bodily systems has a physical form. Even our blood has a form!

Believe it or not, the same energy of the neutrinos in the universe, the god particle in us are our thoughts. That's right! Thoughts are energy! Thoughts have no form and we cannot see thought, right? Yet our thoughts form things. Thoughts are in the mind and the mind is in the brain. The brain has two functions governed by the left and the right brain. The left brain is the "**intellectual**" side. It is the logical thinking side. It thinks a lot and it thinks it knows everything too. Things it doesn't know, it gets frustrated with and becomes fearful of. This is the lower conscious level of the mind. It is the ego and we will refer it as the lower self in this chapter.

On the other hand, the right brain is the "**intelligence**" side. Intelligence means information. Intelligence is the inner knowingness, knowingness is wisdom, and wisdom is commonsense, the sense that is not so common; very few people have it. The right brain is the collective side of the brain, the subconscious, superconscious and supreme consciousness. We are going to refer to this side of the brain as the Higher Self.

The subconscious is innate and is a part of us put there to accept any thought and any belief system and always be in agreement with the conscious mind. It is the consciousness that explores human experiences to learn and grow from creating thoughts, making decisions, with emoting, and producing feelings which the heart accepts.

By now we are fully aware that thoughts become words, words become actions, actions become our character and we are what we believe. Can you see more clearly now how we live our lives based on the belief systems produced by our thoughts? What happens if the belief system is not authentic because it has been altered by other peoples' belief systems and it causes pain and misery? Well, it will deeply affect just about every decision that we make based on the deception that we believe to be true. What we believe becomes programmed into our subconscious, and it will always say yes and agree with what we tell it! Things that we believe, we become! Thoughts literally "matter". Thoughts are energy. The energy of our thoughts become the basis of our actions and life events. We create our own realities through the energy of our own thoughts and belief systems.

Super consciousness is inner knowing, the inner guidance level of consciousness. It is a part of the soul and is so loving. It always has our best interests in mind, but how many of us allow ourselves to tune in to listen to the inner guidance that the super conscious has to offer?

The supreme conscious is Divine Source energy, the spirit that is already perfect, with unconditional love, peace, joy and harmony, but how many people tap into that part of the authentic Divine self and allow themselves to be more Divine? This is why I feel the need to help people understand it.

Both sides of the brain, the lower self and the higher self are talking to us all the time. When we pay more attention to the lower self, the ego in the left brain, its voice becomes louder to us because we give more power to it. On the contrary, if we pay more attention to the higher self, the collective consciousness in the right side of the brain, their voices become louder. We can choose if we will give our power to the right or the left side of our brain, the lower self or the Higher Self.

When we tune in, and become more in tune, we hear those voices in the form of intuition. Intuition means, inner guidance, our inner knowing. We must be aware that they are there, whether we choose to listen to them or not. With the freewill that we have to experience life, we can choose what we want to think, and even Source will not interfere with what we choose to think. This is why it is crucial for us to raise our awareness to become conscious of our thoughts.

The power of our thoughts is the power of Source, it is powerful because the

unconditional love from Source is the supreme
power of the universe. Love gives light and
wherever there is light, there is no darkness.
The power of love heals everything. Now let
me show you how the energy of thoughts works
within us. I will use an analogy with a
comparison between energy and water. Energy
and water operate similarly. Pretend the body
is a water tank. Imagine along with me that we
collect water from all over the world to put in
our tank. What happens when we put all the
water we collected in the tank? The water
become one unit. All is one, right? That's how
energy works in our mind. We become one
with the frequency of any energy we collect in
our mind. What happens if we collect muddy
water from somewhere and put it in our tank?
The rest of the water in the tank will be
contaminated and start getting cloudy, right?

Imagine now that we keep collecting
more and more muddy water and put it in the
tank, the water in the entire tank will become
muddy. Well, thoughts are like that. Imagine
thoughts in our minds being contaminated
with low frequency that is muddy from a habit
of collecting negative thoughts. That is not a
good thing, is it? Again, because thoughts
become words, words become actions, actions
become our character and we are what we
believe. What we believe we become. How
muddy will we be if we keep becoming
entangled with negative thoughts? What kind
of beliefs are in your belief system? Which

thoughts hold light and which ones hold darkness? What is the underlying belief coming into your awareness right now? Do you feel you should keep it or let it go? Learn to be aware of your thoughts and beliefs and choose the ones that best serve you.

The energies in the mind are like the water in the tank, we must keep our energy clean. How do we do that? Very simple! We get rid of the mud and replace it with clean water. Meaning that we clear the negative thoughts from our minds, and we choose to replace them with positive thoughts, positive thinking; resulting in positive belief systems. There is a catch to this! If we do not place a filtering system in the tank, it's going to get dirty again, right? You know how fountains must have filtering systems to keep their water clean? In the same way we need to have a filtering system in our mind. What is that filtering system in the mind that we need to have?

It is **awareness**! We need to have an awareness to filter our thought processes. Within 3 seconds, we can filter the thoughts with our awareness and if we don't like what we find, we get to replace it. We all have the gift of freewill. All of the 7.8 billion-souls on earth have this exact same gift of freewill from the universe. Meaning that nobody can make us think anything that we do not want to think.

Even Source will not interfere with what we choose to think.

When we have "awareness", we can choose to think different thoughts, right? How do we have that awareness? Well, back to the simplicity! It is from practicing meditation! It has been scientifically proven that when we meditate, we take our consciousness to the Alpha level, the first altered state of the mind and at this level, we tap into the pineal gland and we activate the right side of the brain, the collective consciousness of subconscious, superconscious and supreme consciousness that is filled with pure love and wisdom. Within 3 seconds of filtering a thought, we can in an instant assess it and replace it with whatever we choose.

Now let me show you how we know what needs to be changed and how to make those changes. Energies vibrate at different frequencies, right? Okay, let's pretend we have 21 levels of vibrations: **11** being at a neutral level, and **12** to **21** are being high frequency levels. The high frequencies vibrate with the feelings of gratitude, love, peace/harmony, joy, compassion, kindness, acceptance, trust, forgiveness, and non-judgement. These are the vibrations of Divine Source, the divine energy within us in the right brain.

On the contrary, the frequencies from **10** down to **1,** the low vibration of the frequencies from the left side of the brain, carry judgement. Judgement is the muddiest because it carries dominant energy at very low vibration. It seems that the lowest frequencies will have the greatest influence on our thoughts if we don't use our awareness to filter them. It is when we judge ourselves or judge others, that open ourselves up to the frequencies of fear, hatred, anger, resentment, guilt, shame, worry, sadness, and jealousy which lead to disharmony. When we are in disharmony, everything turns dysfunctional on us. These are the frequencies within the left brain that creates mudding emotions. Through our freewill, we can choose what part of the brain we want to give more power to; the left or the right, the divine within us or human side of us, the ego or the collective, the lower self or the higher self. The choice is ours!

These are the options that we need to be aware of. So, when you make choices with every thought that you are aware of, you will have plenty of good options to choose from. I find that the high vibrational options bring joy. All of them are good choices. Obviously, the low frequency options from the ego are poor choices. Remember to catch your thoughts and use your awareness as a filter and to purify the muddy energy with clean energy. Any thought that seems muddy, don't keep it and simply replace it with a clear, clean positive, good thought. It takes only 3 to 7 seconds to do this. By creating your new habit and adoption this new way of being and your entire reality will change dramatically.

Every one of us is very powerful and we are able to co-create our realities with the universe. Any thought that the heart accepts becomes an emotion and emotion turns into feeling. Feeling is the energy force that drives us to connect with the infinite energy in the universe. The universe has no judgement and always lovingly says yes to every vibration that we send out from every feeling and becomes one just like the water in the tank. The UNI (infinite self) and VERSE (the group of little selves of the infinite) become one at this time. There is no judgement of good or bad, right or wrong. The experiences that the UNI has through the VERSE are to learn from the human experiences of being imperfect. This is the purpose of freewill.

The universe will lovingly work its magic like an alchemist, co-creating our reality with each frequency we project. Our creations will be manifested in our reality with help from the universe. If we have a habit of having thoughts that fill us up with fear and our hearts accept it, the emotion of fear becomes a feeling that will be co-created by the universe. The universe says yes, we will co-create more fear for you to experience so we can experience it with you, and of course, there will be more situations that create fear and it will be manifested in our reality. What we think we become.

On the contrary, when we catch a fearful thought and within 3 seconds, we make a change, and make it a loving thought instead, the universe again will say, *"Yes!"* We will co-create more vibrations of love with you in your reality and that too will be manifested. We get to manifest more loving situations in our reality. This is the nature of ONE! All is ONE just like water in the tank, the UNI and the VERSE.

We have about 7.8 billion-souls on earth at this point and we all came onto this beautiful earth to experience human emotions, co-existing to learn and grow, so we can evolve back to Source. We all came in with the exact same gift. The gift of freewill! Even Source will not interfere with what anyone chooses to think. We must utilize the gift of freewill, with the Divine power within us, not with the power of the ego. Remember to practice mindfulness to raise awareness. **Meditate, meditate and meditate!** It is free and it will free you too! Free you from thinking muddy thoughts! Free you from collecting and being like the muddy water in the tank.

We want to think good thoughts for our hearts to accept with the feelings of love, peace, harmony, joy, compassion, kindness and do so with courage and trust. The process of co-creating with the universe requires conscious awareness. We must focus on what we would like to have more of. The universe will help us with those manifestations and we just have to be patient with it. The universe works on divine timing giving us the experiences we attract with our thoughts, beliefs, emotions and feelings.

Now we have a basic understanding of the power that lies within our belief systems. The thought processes in the mind are extremely powerful and it can either build us up or break us down. Many of us process our thoughts under the programming of others based on our upbringing, social standards, and physical environment, as well as schooling, culture, and traditions. Some of the belief systems are more rigid than others. Since we are what we believe, can you imagine how rigid belief systems can cause us more harm than good? What about the traditions or the cultures that have very strict limitations? What kind of belief system do we end up holding on to? Does it build us up or break us down? Perhaps both! It depends on how we project it into our lives and interact with the people around us.

I was born and raised in Thailand and lived there until I was 17 and then moved to the US. That was many moons ago. I realized that Thai tradition and the culture are very different from the US. It took me a while to adapt and adjust to become comfortable with my then new environment. I've lived here in the US long enough now to be more in the flow of the cultural differences, but still have not fully embraced all the differences. I appreciate many of the Thai cultural traditions, although I've never fully embraced them either. I felt like I did not belong anywhere at one point until I found my true self, and now I feel like I belong everywhere. I am a citizen of planet Earth. I'm a unique self, having my own unique experiences. I respect others who also are citizens of Earth, having their unique experiences. Wherever we are is the place where we belong to have our experiences. We just have to be okay with who we are and have peace within us, so we can co-exist and flow with the circumstances in our lives comfortably.

The feeling of not belonging made me feel lonely and misunderstood until I became aware of the truth that I can create my own reality and accept myself from within. The feeling of belonging everywhere happened to me organically. It saved me from drowning in my own old belief system which had created an underlying feeling of sadness and melancholy as I was going through life. I turned off the sense of being on unconscious autopilot and letting life's momentum carry me and turned on my awareness allowing me to choose how I want reality to be for me. I choose to carry my own belief system regardless of where I am or what people think of me. It is a precious treasure that I hold onto as my foundation. It is truly more valuable than everything physical.

Would you rather be in a cage made of gold or be free?

I would very much like with my pure intention to share my insight with you about how we can be one with the universe. The following information may help you understand how we are all absolutely unique, and yet in this uniqueness, there is a similarity in all of us. It is the energy in us which is similar. What we do with it is unique. We are connected energetically to all, but we can choose to have our own unique experience and create our own reality at will through the consciousness and our Divine power within.

In science, the scientists have found that very piece of DNA has a field around it. Every piece of DNA is next to another piece and a field around it has another field around it. All the pieces combined together create a Oneness of consciousness. Consciousness is a state of awareness within self. It is a quantum engine for the body. You can raise your conscious awareness of Oneness and speak to the body as One even though there are hundreds of trillions of energies within it. In DNA, there is a piece of Divine Source, a piece of home. There is a quantum-ness in DNA; intelligence in its consciousness design.

Science has proven that the field around DNA is inter-dimensional. One piece is linked to another and also against one another, creating an interlocking, and over-lapping web of energy. It has an inter-dimensional field that has one address in the universe, and this address has your name on it. The whole body experiences the overlapping of the field of DNA. Those overlapping fields create a larger field that creates a larger field by the time we get to hundreds of trillions of them in the field, we can project light. This light is ready to listen to and serve the body, to heal the body. (The healing light within.)

When you are aware of this power, you can utilize it at will. Anything is possible, knowing that the consciousness in DNA has a divine power (The Higher Self) that is one with the greater power (Divine Source, The Creator) of the cosmos. There is a universal language that we can use to communicate with Oneness, and it is the language of the heart's frequency. The feelings of the heart affect the body, the mind and the soul.

When we carry baggage, the mind projects pain into the heart, the heart feels that pain and the heart projects, the frequency of pain into the body and the soul experiences it through consciousness and sends it out into the universe. People around us can feel that frequency of pain in us and it causes a ripple effect. Like attracts like, we attract more of the same frequency and we experience more of it.

The quantum magnetic field in DNA works as a receiver and each one of us creates this same field within our mind through our thoughts. Thoughts are energy. Thoughts are consciousness. With our freewill we can raise conscious awareness and selectively place the focus of our thinking on thoughts that are positive. That is also choosing light over darkness. When the heart accepts those thoughts, the feelings that the heart accepts will send out magnetic energy from the feeling and it becomes one with the quantum energy field. Just as when we add a drop of water to a water tank, that drop of water becomes an integral part of the rest of the water in the tank.

There is a mechanism by which like attracts like, what we send out, will become a part of a field which attracts the same field of whatever we create in our mind. The energy we resonate with, we attract. We do have the ability to tune the frequency of our resonance through the thoughts, emotions, feelings and beliefs we choose.

Ever since I raised my awareness by accepting my true self, I've lived my life now in a different reality from most people and it is a different reality from what I used to have earlier in my life. I broke away from my old bad habits which created so much trouble and attract more of it into my life. Now I have the new wonderful habit of sending gratitude for everything in any given moment that I bring my awareness to. It doesn't matter if it is big or small. I love and accept myself and appreciate the simplicity that life has to offer. The feelings of love that I have for myself and others are constantly overflowing, and it sends out as a river of light everywhere to everything and everyone.

I get to touch people and therefore, I bring joy, harmony and calmness out in them. People become more balanced when I'm around and I really enjoy creating this kind of reality in my environment. I do not see many issues in life anymore. I only see a lot of opportunities to grow. I do not feel the need to react much to anything since I've practiced non-judgement. I accept everything for what it is and all of us are growing and evolving as much as we allow it. Someone is teaching and learning from somebody. All is well.

As I mentioned in the previous chapter, we are here on Earth for two main life purposes; to evolve further and to be of service to one another. Again, evolve means returning back to something and when you spell the word evolve, e-v-o-l-v-e and from spelling L backward to L-O-V-E. Love! We are evolving back to love, to our own origin of unconditional love. To love is to evolve and when we learn to love unconditionally, we evolve back to the vibration of our origin and that fills us with great harmony, peace, compassion, kindness, and joy as we are returning back to unconditional love. When we are more evolved, we get to be of service to one another more successfully and effectively.

In order to be of service effectively and successfully, we have to be of service to ourselves first. We first must love and accept ourselves. Below are the golden rules to help us with our soul's evolution so we can have more to give to others. There are five crafts that we have the opportunity to master for our soul's evolution; (1) Unconditional love, (2) Compassion, (3) Acceptance, (4) Forgiveness and (5) Trust. These five crafts share the same key principle and it is Non-judgement. To learn these crafts well we must understand the principle of nonjudgement.

To master the craft of **Unconditional love**, we must practice non-judgement. We learn to love ourselves unconditionally, so we don't judge ourselves. We learn to love others unconditionally; and we don't judge them, aware that we are no lesser or greater than one another. We just evolve at a different rate. Remember, there are 4 types of souls: (1) Spiritual and Evolved, (2) Evolved but not Spiritual, (3) Spiritual but not Evolved and (4) neither Evolved nor Spiritual. Because we are here to be of service to one another, the evolved souls that are not spiritual somehow seem to pair up with the spiritual souls that are not evolved. They teach and learn and help one another to become more evolved and more spiritual.

The ones that are evolved and spiritual, who sometimes forget, are able to learn the most from those who are not evolved and not spiritual. The not evolved and not spiritual are giving the opportunity to the evolved and spiritual to master those five crafts I mentioned. We are all teachers and students to each other.

The mastery of **Compassion** requires the same practice of non-judgement. We get to learn to have great compassion for ourselves, therefore, we do not judge ourselves. We learn to have great compassion for others, so we do not judge them.

Acceptance can be mastered with the same principle of non-judgement. We learn to accept ourselves and others as Divine presence having human experiences, we have no need to judge anyone, including ourselves.

Forgiveness is an intense lesson for people to learn, and it requires the very same principle of non-judgement. When we forgive, we are not doing it for others as much as we are doing it for ourselves. We must forgive to set ourselves free from the burden of hurt, pain and misery. We have freewill to either choose to hold onto something or let go of it. Also, when we forgive ourselves, we liberate ourselves from the painful feelings of guilt or shame that do not complement us at all. Mistakes are only part of the lessons we must learn and evolve through. When we do not judge, we do not react; and when we do not hold grudges, we do not have anyone to forgive. Forgiveness is a magical mastery in itself.

Trust! When we trust this process, it is much easier to practice non-judgement. These are the five crafts we need to master in order to advance us in our soul evolution. They allow us to evolve back to love, the unconditional love that has no judgement. It is the circle of the cycle of the experience of what it is like not to be perfect, to then grow and expand back to wholeness of LOVE and light. It is the purity of love that heals everything. Love gives light and wherever there is light, there is no darkness. When we are more evolved, we are able to be of service to humanity and to one another more effectively. Imagine as we are being of service to others, we always want to give our all, but if our all is based on a finite amount of love within us, we do not have a lot to give. When we do not have much self-love, and only give love to others, we eventually feel depleted.

When we have self-love and maintain it, we are less likely to become depleted helping others. We need to listen to our own bodies, respecting our own boundaries and look within ourselves. Give ourselves the hugs and practice having connection with self by looking at ourselves in the mirror, smile and talk to self with compassion and kindness. Talk to the person in the mirror with the feeling that the Divine self is talking to the physical body of self. Thank the body, the mind, and the soul lovingly, for carrying on the unique journey to experience imperfection and the opportunity to evolve back to love.

Tell the person you are looking at in the mirror what you want to hear and how proud you are of your willingness to keep learning and improving yourself. Say *"I love you"* to yourself often. Do not wait for anyone to tell you. You are the one who first must love and accept yourself. You are the most important person in the world. There is only one of you to experience you for your own growth.

Love yourself with all your heart and let the feeling of love overflow to others naturally. Be conscious of the thoughts that your heart accepts. Create more love in your heart. Be loving. Be kind to yourself and let the energy of your best self, overflow to others. Contribute to this beautiful world by flowing love into it. Enhance the beauty of the world by helping raise the vibration of Earth. Love is all we need. Love is free, but the value of love is priceless.

We co-exist to enhance the ability of one another to grow and love complementing the growth in all of us. Love yourself and let it overflow to others naturally. Have fun with life. Make lemonade from the lemons that life throws at you. Create a habit of looking at things from the perspective of light and enjoy the learning you experience from all your relationships with others. Have a good relationship with yourself first and offer that same feeling to others. Create the frequency of love within yourself and give it as a gift to others.

We must diligently work on ourselves, learn to love ourselves and overflow it to others. Practice kindness and have compassion for self and others. Forgive ourselves and everyone to set ourselves free to liberate ourselves from hurt, pain and misery. Accept ourselves for who we are and accept others for who they are. Practice having patience. Send gratitude to everything that we have and to all the lessons learned from everyone involved. Trust the learning process that there is a divine purpose for every circumstance. Be in a state of peace, joy and harmony and become balanced and wholesome within.

Every time we are being of service to others, we are giving our all, and we feel energized. What goes around comes around. As we give, we receive. That is the law of the universe. It is the law of oneness and frequency. The energy frequency we emit we attract. Imagine the world we live in and see each one of us contributing by bringing love, peace, joy and harmony to our circle of friends, family and colleagues, one beautiful soul at a time; how beautiful this world will be for us.

Remember to take the personal responsibility to make some good changes to make a difference and to just BE. Be in the flow of loving kindness and enjoy experiencing life together. Enjoy the process of making mistakes to learn and grow without beating ourselves up. Look back at mistakes and see what we can learn and grow from. See if we make the same mistake again, or if we do become aware of the patterns we created and focus on the change that is needed with courage. Self-respect is essential. Be respectful to self, so we do not take ourselves down in vibration with muddied negative emotion. Be kind and work on forgiving your "self" and others, then move on. This is how we can grow spiritually. Learn from life's experiences and you will not repeat the same mistakes.

Many people have a habit of worrying a lot. They worry about the what if. What if I don't have this? What if I don't have that? What if this happens? What if that happens? We need to have an awareness of these kinds of thoughts because they will create a bad habit of always worrying about the future, putting us in a constant state of anxiety. Worrying attracts and creates the experiences we want to avoid. Understand that any of the what if's that don't serve you, don't happen unless your mind focuses on them. If they do happen, they are created by you focusing on them.

Even if what you fear happens, it is only a problem if you perceive it to be a problem. Stress and stress hormones are created by our own perceptions. You create your own stress and can choose to not create it. We can perceive an event as a learning opportunity to foster much needed change. The future is filled with the unknown and the unknown can create fear. Fear is not even real. It is an illusion, a product of the mind. If we give the power of thought to fear and perceive it to be real, it will be as real as we perceive it to be. Our mind is that powerful!

Fear is something that we all face. If we give our power to it, and live our lives in fear, it will block us and prevent us from moving forward. Fear also influences decision making. When we make any decision based on fear, we are blocking ourselves from seeing some of the good options that may give us better outcomes. It narrows our vision and our perception. We must overcome all fears and allow ourselves to live our lives with all the possibilities within the beauty of our truth. We cannot do that if fear has control over us. I have a few stories to share with you about how certain fears were affecting my life, but most importantly, I wish to show you how I overcame them. My intention of telling these stories is to inspire you and help build your courage to overcome fear in ways you personally experience it.

My fear of dogs – I remember the time when I was afraid of dogs. It last for decades. It started when I was bitten by the same dog twice when I was only 8 years old. The worst part about it was that the dog belonged to a relative. During that time, I was living with my grandmother. Her house was built on family's land that belonged to our ancestors, two brothers who were once prominent during their lives. They had lots of children from many 'Sister Wives'. This land was passed down as an inheritance for multiple families related to one another. Ten families built their homes in this compound and I could not tell then and still to this day cannot figure out exactly what relationship we had with one another. All I knew was that all of them shared the same family trees (two trees from the two brothers).

I remember very well having to go in and out of the compound through a long, tall, white wooden fence. This fence separated the families from the rest of the neighborhood. The neighborhood street was named after one of the brothers. You could not see the compound from outside of the fence. I was told that my grandmother was married to one of the children of the two brothers whom I'd never met because he passed away before I was born.

My mother carried his last name - the same name as the estate name posting on the tall white fence. That was the only thing I knew about that made me a part of the family tree. My grandma's house was built in the back of the estate. I had to walk past all of the homes in order to enter or exit through the main gate. One of the homes that belonged to the people who I called auntie and uncle, located at the very front of the estate. I was comfortable going there on a regular basis to play with her children since they were my relatives.

One day, her family found a dog on the street and decided to adopt him and raise him as their pet. This dog was a barker. He barked at everything in sight. Her family liked it because they felt like he was a good watch dog for the family, but I did not feel the same way at all. Actually, I stopped going inside their home because I did not feel comfortable being barked at. I remember the day when I was walking toward the tall white wooden fence to go out to the neighborhood, the dog ran toward me and kept barking at me. I jumped and ran from him because I was frightened by him. My fear of this dog increased more and more each time this happened and I'm sure he could sense it.

Every time I walked near the area, he would run toward me and keep barking at me. I was already frightened by him and did not know if he would attack me or not. I would fearfully jump, scream and run from him every single time. Auntie said he was a friendly dog and that he would never harm anyone, and she suggested that I make friends with him. Being a little girl who was already frightened by his approach, I preferred to run away from him rather than make friends with him.

Fear kept accumulating and the dog become more and more exhilarated by my increased fear, as if I were his prey he was hunting in the wild. One day, on a rainy day, when he was barking as he was running toward me, I placed an umbrella in front of me. I was hoping that it would guard me from him just in case he attacked me. My aunt told me that because I did that, the dog felt threatened by me. Therefore, when he saw me the next time, he didn't even bother to bark, but ran directly to bite me. It wasn't a bad bite, but the fear of him had accumulated and heightened to the point that I refused to go out from that side of the home. I snuck out the other door on the opposite side of my other relative's home which was a small private entrance, not the main entrance for everyone.

It was inconvenient, but I was too afraid to face that dog again. This went on for months until the day of the next incident. The day that the dog found me standing and playing alone in one of my relative's home. This home was adjacent to my grandma's house in the back of the property. I felt something wet and cold touching my leg, so I turned around to see what it was and there it was. The dog was sniffing my leg.

The moment I was aware of what it was, I screamed at the top of my lungs. The dog was frightened by my reaction. We frightened each other. When I turned my body around and screamed, he bit down on the front inner part of my calf muscle. It was a pretty bad bite this time and from those moments onward, a phobia of being around dogs was instilled in me. I would scream, run and hide from just hearing any barking around me. It took much joy away from me. I couldn't live a normal life like everyone else. When I became an adult, I promised myself that one day I would overcome this fear. I couldn't stand living life like that forever, but I did not know when I would be brave enough to face it.

I really had to do something about it, and I made a decision to face that fear in my mid 30's. I came up with a plan to find the way to warm myself up to overcoming my fear. My brilliant plan was to adopt a cute puppy and raise him as my pet, in hoping to take my time working on my emotional wound and my fear of being around dogs. That day finally came. The day I felt ready to take on the task of raising a puppy of my own. I gave myself the gift of a Pomeranian puppy. I named him Pommie because he looked like a little pom pom. He was cute, adorable and loving. I loved him and learned to trust him. I knew in my heart that he would not turn on me or on my family.

Pommie became an important member of our family. He became a part of our daughter's life soon after she was born. He often was in the bed with me and our baby girl during our leisure time. He was so good to the baby and it was a comforting feeling for me. It was this good feeling that helped prepare me to be able to eliminate my fear of dogs in the future. Pommie taught me that not all dogs are scary. Thanks to Pommie, I learned to have more peace around dogs. He was the biggest help. I'm glad I was committed to face that fear by raising him from the puppy stage.

Consequently, it gave me an opportunity to overcome my phobia. I no longer have adrenaline shooting out to make me scream or panic from being around dogs anymore. That outcome was truly a blessing. This was a very big deal to me, and it inspired me to put more work into dealing with my other fears. I decided that I would conquer other fears, anything that took my joy away, I would face them as they popped up.

My fear of heights – I became braver after I was successful at clearing the phobia of dogs from my life. My fear of heights became my next endeavor. I used the same tactic by promising myself that one day when I'm ready,

I will conquer this fear too. That day came, when Janet, my dear friend, took me to a beautiful indoor botanical garden in Washington D. C. The set up was beautiful, and in order to get the most out of its beauty, we needed to walk up steps that took us to the top of the room. I realized that I'd just came across an opportunity to confront my fear of heights at that moment, and I was ready to deal with it head on. I did what I knew best – I talked myself into becoming ready. I felt brave enough to take my first step and I kept focusing on moving forward, step by step until I was on the top floor.

Voila, it worked! When I got up there, my fear of heights dissipated. I looked down to see the entire set up of the special creation for the holidays. It was spectacular! I was proud of myself and I wanted to pat myself on the back for being courageous. I was able to overcome my fear of heights which had held me back from experiencing magnificent beauty like this for a long period of time. I was proud of my achievement and was determined to do more self-work in other areas. I was becoming more courageous with each victory.

My fear of drowning – At this point, I was ready to take on a bigger task. I was already in my mid-thirties, and I didn't even know how to swim yet. Again, I promised myself that, one day, when I'm ready, I will take a swimming lesson to overcome my fear of drowning. Although, I couldn't swim, I wanted all my children to learn how to swim at a very young age because I believe it is an important skill to have. I arranged for my son to take his baby sister for a swimming lesson for me, because I did not want to be in the water. By the way, my son was 13 years old and his baby sister was only one year of age.

I did not like the way I felt, and I decided that it was time for me to face this fear too. I did not like the feeling that her big brother had to take her to a swimming lesson instead of me, her mother. I signed up for a separate swimming lesson for myself. I was mentally ready and again was determined to overcome that fear no matter what it took.

To my surprise, because I was mentally ready, I could swim across the whole length of the swimming pool from one end to the other during my first lesson. I believed that it must be the power of my mind which carried me through. I was proud of my courage and have not had any fear of drowning ever since. There is one thing I must mention, and it makes me laugh telling you about it. I could only swim while I kept my face down in the water. I could hold my breath while I was swimming across the pool. Because of that, I never learned how to breath properly like other people do, but it was good enough for me. I do not like being in the water that much anyway. I do not like the feeling of getting cold in the water and the smell of the chlorine.

At least I achieved my goal of overcoming fear of drowning and that meant everything to me. Ever since I have released all the known fears that I had in the past, I've been able to live life with much more joy and have participated in more activities with others without holding myself or others back.

Furthermore, as I started to live my life without fear, I became calmer, and more balanced. Acquiring this quality actually ended up saving my life. A life-threatening incident happened recently. My family and I were on a vacation. During that time, I took a handful of supplements all at once with ice cold water. I normally would take them with room temperature water and of course, not all at once. Some of the pills would not go down properly and were stuck in my airway.

I wondered if it was because of the cold drink, some of the pills would not go down properly. I was aware of what was happening to me. I calmly told my daughter to grab me a glass of water and I kept drinking it. I was hoping that it would help me to get them down my throat, but it didn't work. I realized how this incident could really end up in a tragedy, but I did not panic. Instead, I was able to handle it calmly. I got up to walk toward the front of the room, and my body started to assist itself. I felt the need to vomit, so I ran into the bathroom and let my body take care of itself. My body's own instincts pushed the supplements stuck in my throat out of my body.

Fortunately, I was able to purge them out, and was able to avoid the potential tragedy of choking to death that day while my daughter watched. It was a good thing that I was able to stay calm the entire time. I realized that if I had begun to panic, it would have created tensions in my body to the point that my throat would have shut and completely blocked my airway.

Fortunately, I successfully avoided the worst case-scenario. This incident taught me a few things. I've learned that having an ability to keep calm in the face of an emergency can truly prevent a situation from going from bad to worse and possibly turn tragic. Also, since then, I've been taking my time with my supplements, not all at once and drinking plenty of water with while swallowing them. I am more careful now because I realized that I might not be as lucky next time, if it happens again.

These were some of the personal experiences I wanted to share with you. My intention is to help you relate to how we can overcome fear if we really work on it. Also, it is a helpful reminder that practicing meditation regularly can keep us balanced and allow us to utilize our powerful minds to protect us from harm. I suggest that you apply the knowledge you've gained from reading chapter 3, The Higher Vision of Meditation, and chapter 4, The Higher Vision of the Power of the Mind, to help you build the strong foundation that you need. When life throws you a curve ball, it will be easier for you to catch it, or avoid it and simply have fun with it.

When we are present, aware, and in the moment without fear, we see more, feel more and we can sense more easily how to navigate the situation at hand. Chapter 3, The Higher Vision of Meditation demonstrated how you can simply and naturally add a meditation practice into your daily routine. It is simple, but extremely effective. It will help raise your awareness and awaken calmness within you, the quality that you need to have, in dealing with any circumstances, in any situation. Chapter 4, The Higher Vision of the Power of the Mind, described and demonstrated how powerful our mind is and how we can choose to utilize it.

Again, it is simple, and it serves as an effective guideline for you. It will make it easier for you to be able to identify the power within you and know what you can do with it. The sense of knowing and being in your own powerful best self is an important tool, and that will help you in navigating your own life and supporting others to do the same. I'd like to also remind readers again, that fear is an illusion. It is a product of the mind. We have the power to create it or discard it through our own freewill.

Remember how powerful our mind is and **your power and ability** to co-create our reality with the universe with our emotions and feelings. Focus on each moment and utilize the power of now. Co-create what you want in your reality in every minute instead of creating more of what you don't want.

The power of NOW works magically. It is about choosing to focus on the present moment and allowing each moment to be your very best moment. Present means gift! Give this gift to yourself by focusing on the power of each moment without thinking of the past or future. Anything that already happened one minute or millions of minutes before is not happening anymore in this present moment.

Also, the future is not in this moment yet. Since the future is filled with the unknown and the unknown creates fear, why should we bring fear that is not even real into the present moment to interfere with our best moment, which we are having right now? Focusing on the present moment. There is no need to bring in the past nor future that will interfere with the gift of being in the present of NOW! This "now" moment is a gift of self-love. Give this gift to yourself again and again and do so now.

Focus on every present moment as it is the most precious gift you can give yourself. Since neither the past nor the future are in the present moment, we can focus on each moment and the power that the now moment has. We remember now that we are a Divine Presence having human experiences. Claim your power and embody it. Be in the presence of the great I AM! Claim that I AM, a divine presence having human experiences. I am all love, peace and joy. Say this mantra to yourself and feel what you are saying, **"I am co-creating my reality with these vibrations that I choose to be. I shall not bring the past nor the future into my present moment and I choose to just be, be in the presence of my divine authentic self and I trust that each moment, I give my best to every moment of my life."** <u>Claim this self-worth and OWN it!</u> It is your Divine right!

So, allow your present moment to be in the power of now and focus on remembering that we all have divine energy within us. Remember that we can co-create and manifest anything through the feelings from the thoughts that our heart accepts. Utilize the gift of freewill, remember to co-create with high vibrations at the highest frequency of Divine power with love, peace, joy and harmony. Make it habit. Have an awareness of your ability to co-create what you want as your reality.

Focus on ABUNDANCE instead of lack! LOVE instead of hatred or fear! JOY instead of sadness! COMPASSION instead of anger! HARMONY instead of disharmony! GRATITUDE for everything that you have instead of complaining about things that you don't have or want to have more of.

Gratitude carries the highest vibration. When we co-create with the universe with the vibration of gratitude, we will have more and more abundance to be grateful for. A greater abundance of love, good relationships, peace, joy, harmony and even greater abundance of money, which will be manifested with the power of the mind. It is like placing an order to the universe with pure intention and then just waiting for it to be delivered by the universe when we are ready.

Speaking of abundance of money, some people have a habit of thinking of lack and complain and worry about not having enough and those are the people who are not aware that they are manifesting more lack into their realities. When they shift their thought process into the thoughts of abundance and their heart accepts, all of a sudden, more doors open up to them and help them achieve and create more abundance. This is the law of attraction of the universe. Like attracts like. What we think,

229

believe, emote and feel attracts our experiences and creates our reality. We are what we choose to become a part of, and we are the maker of it in our own reality!

This concept of quantum energy of Source is so powerful! The ball is in your court now. Utilize your freewill and choose the highest frequency option. The choices are obvious; LOVE vs. hatred, COURAGE vs. fear, JOY vs. sadness, HARMONY vs. disharmony, COMPASSION vs. anger, ACCEPTANCE vs. guilt or shame, ABUNDANCE vs. lack, FORGIVENESS vs. grudges, KINDNESS vs. hostility and so on. Remember to choose the best options with your freewill and to remember to JUST BE! Be in the presence of love, peace, joy, harmony and JUST BE! Make it simple! The universe makes things so simple. We do not need to complicate things anymore.

The energy of the universe is within us, in our own DNA and is allowing us to choose our human experiences. The experiences may be different, but all is one. We can choose to experience difficulty or simplicity. It is up to us to choose of our own freewill. Source always loves all of us unconditionally. We can learn what it is like being outside of love and we can find our way back to the Source of love. I know it works from my own experience and from witnessing the experiences of others.

Making changes within our belief system to be more loving, and kind to ourselves and one another creates miracles. We become more productive, living lives with much more joy and the ability to self-heal through the understanding of the cause and effect that occurs from the interaction of our thoughts, emotions and feelings. This reality can be yours if you choose to apply it and make it work for you rather than against you.

Most importantly, this will definitely raise your vibration and that will help you with your ascension process and in making the transition into the New Earth. In the next chapter I will share more about this and explain the New Earth, so you have a better understanding of it, and can make some important choices enabling you to be part of it if you choose.

Chapter Seven:
The Higher Vision
of the New Earth

I believe it is important to inform my wonderful readers about the ascension process of our planet because it does have an effect on every human on earth. This is a grand opportunity for humanity to shift its consciousness during this great awakening of souls. It is beneficial to know about our direct or indirect contributions and how they will affect the outcomes of this process. What we do or don't do, and how we operate within our hearts and minds has a profound effect on the collective consciousness, also affecting the timeline of this event.

We all are a part of One - - Oneness of Source energy. We are like fish in an enormous tank. When the water in the tank is contaminated, the fish will begin to suffocate and eventually will not be able to survive in it. We have been energetically polluting our own tank with fear and hatred - creating conflicts that led to wars; projected hurt and pain to one another unconsciously because of the indifference of our belief systems - the belief systems that were programmed by others.

Humanity are like the fish in Mother Earth's tank. The tank needs to be cleansed or eventually it will need to be replaced. Mother Earth, Gaia, has been doing just that. As she is actively cleansing the earth, she is also working on her creation with the help of the universe and is creating a new tank for us (the New Earth). It is being done at a vibrational level. This information may be mind-bending for some of us, but if we open our minds and our hearts to explore it, we have nothing to lose, but much to gain. We can choose to do nothing and observe it, or perhaps start making some changes that will reward us all.

I already explained in detail in Chapter six how every choice that we make affects both ourselves and one another. Therefore, each one of us is responsible for keeping our energies clean. It is important to have an awareness of the thinking patterns that affects our mind, body and spirit so we can focus on the inner work necessary to stay in harmony. Practicing meditation alone will help raise and maintain the level of our awareness. It helps us to be in touch with our best selves and become more in tuned with our thoughts. If we don't like the feel of a thought, we can simply change it and replace it with pleasant ones that we like. The pleasant feeling that is created from the thoughts that the heart accepts are the vehicle that plays the most important role in this process. It is the key to open the door to the New Earth.

Feelings of love, compassion, gratitude, joy, and harmony are the energies of the New Earth. When we vibrate at that level of frequency, we are automatically in alignment with the New Earth. The high vibrations are extreme opposites from the low vibrations, and they cannot share the same space. In order for us to be a part of the New Earth, we must be proactive and choose to vibrate at the same frequency. We have freewill to choose! We can choose to be a high vibrational being and be energetically aligned with the New Earth and live life in harmony with no war, hatred, fear or dis-functional behaviors.

It is helpful to understand that Gaia is a sentient being and she has consciousness. She is also an experimental planet. The original plan was to see what would happen if freewill was given to the people of the World. In this regard, Gaia has suffered a great deal while humanity keeps making choices that create disharmony, throwing things out of balance. What has happened in the past century has brought concern to the guardians of the cosmos. Especially the idea of nuclear weapons that have a potential to eliminate life on Earth and it cause a ripple effect on the rest of the planets in the Solar system.

It would take an entire book to cover significant detail on the subject. If you would like to learn more about it, I recommend the well written book, The Three Waves of

Volunteers and The New Earth by Dolores Cannon. In this book she shares the information she learned from the Source of knowledge through her hypnosis clients. I highly recommend this book for anyone who would like to obtain greater depth of information on the subject.

Gaia has shifted her consciousness into two. Her old consciousness is still in the 3rd dimension (the old earth), letting people experience lives in the lower densities and low vibrations that they have created. She has evolved her consciousness, become an ascended planet, vibrating in higher vibrations of the 5th dimension (the New Earth)[12]. She is given the same opportunity to anyone who wants to evolve and ascend with her. She is assisting all of the people (the fish in her tank) who choose to take part in this process with her, and she kindly accepts the freewill of those who do not wish to do so at this time. She respects everyone's freewill.

Gaia has been busy cleansing her body, this beautiful planet, of the mess that humanity created. She is resilient and she knows that everything that has been happening, had to happen. How do I know this? Well, this might sound bizarre to you, but what I'm about to tell

---

[12] Cannon, D. (2011*). The Three Waves of Volunteers and The New Earth.* Ozark Mountain Publishing Inc.: New York.

you is my truth. I had an opportunity to have a dialogue with Gaia during the time when I helped one of my clients under Quantum Hypnosis with his health issues. This experience validated it for me.

This person had suffered left leg pain for several years. No doctors or healers were able to help him release it. He also had a few other health issues that lingered on for decades. He was hoping that having a QHHT session with me would help him understand the root causes and perhaps heal himself of his issues. After several hours of our pre-hypnosis talk, we were ready to proceed to the next step with hypnosis. We had a smooth ride under hypnosis, he went under easily and was able to eliminate the pain in his right arm that had been there for 30 years. The cause of this issue was revealed to him and I was astonished by the reason.

He also received lots of answers to his questions from the collective consciousness during our session. A lot was going on during that time, but I wish to focus my attention directly towards one phenomenal experience that helped me validate my knowledge of the New Earth. I will need to turn my focus back to the core story now to talk about my personal experience with the New Earth.

In this event, the Higher Self was called in to help him with everything he needed. It was to my surprise that 'they' were able to help him with everything he requested, except the pain in his left leg. 'They' told us that this pain was not his. It belonged to Mother Earth. It was out of his freewill that he chose to take on her pain and 'they' could not override it. 'They' explained that he is a warrior and he incarnated here on Earth with an intention to help her combat the dark forces, and because of his great empathy, he chose to help her by holding her pain. The Higher Self suggested that we talk to Mother Earth and ask for help.

After I thanked the Higher Self, I asked to speak with Mother Earth. Gaia came through right away and she asked, **"Which Earth would you like to speak to?"** I was extremely excited as I replied to her, *"Oh yes, I forgot that you have two consciousnesses now. May I speak to the one that could help him with this matter please?"* and she replied, **"It will be me. I'm the old earth."** This dialogue was bizarre to me. Gaia, my client and I were having a three-way conversation, and I truly enjoyed it.

When Gaia talked to me or to him, the voice sounded feminine and when he was talking as himself, his voice became masculine again. I engaged in our conversation for a while, but later on it was a time for me to step aside and just listen to their conversation.

Gaia said to him, *"This is not your pain. It is my pain. Everything that has been happening has to happen. I'm working on the cleansing process. Don't worry, I am resilient. I know you are here as a warrior and you are here to help battle the dark forces, but your work will be done to greater effect if you do it in the New Earth. Release my pain and go do your work in the New Earth."* He graciously complied with her request, so I thanked the Old Earth and asked to speak with the New Earth.

Shortly after, the New Earth came in to talk to us, and at that moment, my client put one of his hands on the wall while he brushed his other hand on the hypnosis bed. He described all the beauty and peaceful feelings of being part of the New Earth. It was a precious moment and memorable for me to experience that with him.

It was absolutely magical! No words can describe the feeling! The New Earth talked to him with her gentle voice and told him that she knew he was here to help the Earth fight the war with the dark forces, but there is no war in the New Earth. And that he could still help her by waking people up to their truth.

He complied with Gaia with his kindhearted nature. After he chose to let go of her pain, his leg gradually became better and better. He left our session feeling satisfied and in awe of his experience. He was so pleased that he referred his colleague and the colleague's wife who lived in Canada to see me for their own sessions. They were so inspired by his experience that they wanted to have QHHT experiences of their own. Endorsing me and QHHT to his friends let me know just how profoundly he was affected by his experience with Gaia.

This session was done almost ten years ago, but I still remember those moments like they happened yesterday. This session was highly memorable for me indeed. This is how I know that Gaia is resilient, and she is in the process of ongoing cleansing, cleaning up the mess that humanity has created in her and has forgiven all who have done harm to the Earth. As the clean-up continues, she is making a transition. She is evolving and becoming an ascended planet. Ascending from the Old Earth to the New Earth.

It was to my good fortune that I too, had a personal experience with the New Earth while under hypnosis. This occurred in my hotel room in Arkansas as my colleague and I were exchanging our sessions during the practice exercise following our instruction of the advanced techniques from the level 2 training with Dolores. In my session, I was shown as being an observer from the Cosmos watching the two Earths going through an event. There were two spheres of Earth consciousness that attached to one another. The top consciousness was bright, and the bottom was dark.

As the illumination became brighter and brighter and expanded in size, the bottom dark consciousness kept shrinking and became more and more dense. It was an astonishing experience and it brings me much joy to replay my vision. I almost forgot about it, but the memory of this beautiful experience kept showing up in my mind. I'm so glad to be able to share it with you here and now.

It is really happening! The concept of the new earth is found in most religions and spiritual traditions. It symbolizes a shift in consciousness. In Christianity the shift is called the rapture and the second coming of Christ (the coming of higher consciousness). In Hinduism and Jainism, the shift is signified by Samvartaka fire, and transitioning from the Kali Yuga to the Satya Yuga. Native Americans refer to it as the shift of the 7th fire and rainbow Prophecy. In new age spirituality it is referred to as ascension, ascending in consciousness from the ego mind to the heart and soul, to the vibration of love and joy.

For reference David Wilcock shares the different points of view in detail in several of his videos including the 2019 movie, "The

Cosmic Secret[13]." The book "Hamlet's Mill[14]"
by Santillana and Dechend describes how 35
religions and spiritual traditions indicate a
change occurring on earth at the end of a great
cycle of 25,000-26,000 years and occurring in
the current period.

This is a cycle of her own soul evolution
that Gaia is taking part in. She is finishing up
her last cycle of a Kali Yuga and is transitioning
into a Satya Yuga. In Sanskrit Kali means
Darkness, Satya means Truth and Yuga means
Era/Age. Let me introduce this concept to you
the way that I understand it. I was taught this
concept when I was growing up in Thailand.
The foundation was already there from my
upbringing as a child. I just had to do a little
more research so I could put the concepts into
writing in a cohesive way. The following is the
concept.

There are 4 Yugas in the earth cycle, (1)
Satya Yuga, (2) Treta Yuga, (3) Dvapara Yuga
and (4) Kali Yuga. I will describe only the two
most important Yugas that we are in the midst
of (Kali Yuga and Satya Yuga). This
information may help you to better understand
the ancient beliefs and their teachings of the

---

[13] Reference for movie, *"The Cosmic Secret"*
https://www.imdb.com/title/tt11167116/
[14] Santillana, G. & Dechend, H. (1969). *Hamlet's Mill: An Essay
Investigating the Origins of Human Knowledge and Its
Transmission Through Myth*. Gambit: Boston.

change in consciousness associated with the soul evolution of humanity.

In this Kali Yuga that we are in right now, the realities are not pleasant. The majority of the people during this Yuga are not spiritually advanced and they openly display animosity towards each other. During Kali Yuga people seem to lack moral responsibility becoming addicted to intoxicating substances and strong sexual desires that drown their consciousness. Mutual respect is rare, and people are riding unconsciously on the wheel of karma.

In this Yuga, people seem to have amnesia. They don't remember the truth about the divine power within themselves. Although, we are in the era of the Kali Yuga right now, I'm delighted to inform you that the end of the darkness, the destruction of this old age of Kali Yuga is about to end. We are going through this cycle and transitioning to the Satya Yuga, the age of truth and perfection. Kali Yuga represents the Old Earth and Satya Yuga represents the New Earth. They are different words for the same phenomenon. Gaia is ascending from the Old Earth into the New Earth and we are on the living bridge crossing over to a new age.

What will happen to us? Well, we must do our self-work to ascend with her of course. In this new energy of Satya Yuga, humanity will experience equality. The truth of our Divine selves will be revealed to us when we start looking within ourselves. Of course, because our divine power already exists within us, we just need to claim it. Our job is to remember that we have it. Claim it and own it. It is easy and as simple as I showed you in the last chapter.

Satya Yuga is the best state for humanity to be in and it is perfect timing to start the New Earth. Move away from fear and turn it into love, sorrow into joy, turn competition into cooperation; and there will be no dis-ease because mankind will be able to attain its Divine essence and live lives in truth. People will interact with one another in peace, joy and harmony. We will be able to live life with one another in honesty and in truth. Religion will consist of teachings of the truth of the new energy, if there is a desire to have religion at all. The leaders will demonstrate honesty and be in union with the Divine Presence. The children who are born during this era will be wise and in possession of divine, innate wisdom.

I would like to help people understand and prepare themselves well so they can open themselves up to the new Source energy. Divine consciousness is beaming down on the entire earth at this point. In order to embrace this energy, we need to raise our vibrations to match it. Many of us have done this successfully. I've witnessed many people who have already shifted their consciousness into this level. Some of them graciously came onto my weekly radio show "Get It Straight from the Source" as guests and shared their experiences of the ultimate changes they made that have improved their lives.

Their changes have a ripple effect like a lit candle which continues to light more and more other candles. It is very inspiring to witness these changes through my work. I believe that this book will serve as a key tool to help anyone who is ready to ascend with Gaia to do so. Scot, the editor, said he raised his own vibration tremendously while supporting me with the creation of this book. He has now ascended with Gaia. The change of his energy has influenced the dynamic of his family to be even more loving and increased their ability to understand and accept one another. It is a gift for me to witness and experience this shift in him that has raised the vibrations of his inner circle in a profound way. He feels that this book is a gift to humanity. We feel that the energy of the information given in this book has a wonderful uplifting vibration that engages readers into flow and inspires them.

How this book was developed demonstrates the energy of the New Earth. I felt the need to share this vital information on how to liberate one's own consciousness and live in alignment with Love and our own divine nature. Scot felt the same calling and was excited to support my efforts by editing this book. This book was created as a gift to help others. We grew and became more in tune with love and joy through the experience. The intention is to inspire people who read this book to raise their own vibration and naturally help others to do the same. It is a virtuous cycle of positive energy where we support one another. That is how love flows. That is how love overflows to others.

This reality is available to anyone. You are already in this world. Now, if you choose, you can enter this reality of consciousness, awareness, joy divine connection and love. This is why I must bring awareness to those who are not aware of this big event. I wish to see humanity become more aware and more awake to this ongoing transition and what is available to us. We just have to choose to ride this wave and be a part of this new energy. Gaia is graduating to become an ascended planet. She is shedding the old energy and releasing all past karma that we created. We can do the same thing. We all have the exact same opportunity to progress along with her. To accept the opportunity, we must let go of anything that no longer serves us and most importantly practice forgiveness.

Just choose to drop the karma. Forgiveness is an easy way to clear karma. When we forgive, we set ourselves free, so we will no longer have karmic accounts with others. We can choose to jump off the karmic wheel and let others work themselves out of their own karma. All is well, and yes, it is that easy. Do not complicate things any longer. The universe makes things very easy for us. Let's be in the flow with the universe and reward ourselves with a new life, a new reality that is compatible with the energy of the New Earth. The old energy has to be cleansed before the new energy can be harnessed.

Most of us grew up in the old belief system. We share many experiences of Kali Yuga and as we are making the transition to the Satya Yuga, the old energy of Kali Yuga can no longer be sustained. The old way of living life in competition— ego-based, fear-based, materialistic, inflexible, resistant to self-growth, destroying nature and misusing of power— all of these old ways of operating must be eliminated.

These old ways will be ending with the graduation of Gaia to the New Earth. We must release and let go of the old thought processes and the old energy. They will obviously hold us back from ascending as a group of souls. If we choose not to release the old thought processes and energies, Gaia will respect our freewill, but we will not be able to live life in the energy of the New Earth. The old energy that carries the old belief system will not be allowed to ascend with her and those people will be left behind with what they have created in their own realities. It doesn't matter where we live in the world, or who we are or what cultures we are part of; we are citizens of this planet and all of us have the exact same opportunity to ascend to the New Earth.

This can be done as simply as utilizing our freewill and allowing ourselves to raise our vibration to the quantum level. Become pure with our loving hearts. Be kind and be compassionate toward self and others. Find the honest truth within ourselves. Coming to know the Divine self is the key and it will unlock all doors to freedom. The door to ascension is waiting to be opened with that key, which you already hold within your heart.

Everything is changing all the time and this ultimate change is much needed. The change of the energy of Earth and everything in it is essential. The evolution of Gaia is progressing, and we must do our part so we can graduate with Gaia. She will cooperate with us, nurture us along and celebrate with us in the New Earth. We must have this important awareness and that is to know the power of love of Divine Source within Oneself.

Reevaluate everything! Be more awake, more aware of the new consciousness within the new belief system so we can claim the DIVINE POWER within ourselves. Be more loving to yourself and others; be in harmony with self, with nature, with animals and all that co-exist with us and around us. This is who we are at our best. We need to avoid thinking negative thoughts and stop being hostile toward one another.

Life is so much simpler and more fun when we get along and support one another. When we have peace in our hearts, we will interact with one another peacefully, joyfully and lovingly. Choose to ride this new wave of consciousness that is beaming down to the entire earth. This is Source consciousness that will free us from the old energy in the Kali Yuga and help us make the transition into the new energy in the Satya Yuga with Gaia. We are an integral part of the infinite energy. Consciousness is a quantum energy, a part of our DNA. It is the quantum particle of DNA that may not be understood by science yet. The shift of this great awakening is an opportunity to change DNA with conscious intent. An epiphany of the god particles, the love and light, the Divine presence inside will allow the change at the level of the cellular structure.

Consciousness is a part of that quantum energy of the spirit that is divine and infinite. We are not the body. We are not the mind. We are not the emotions. We are not the feelings. We are experiencing creation through this physical body. We co-create everything in our own reality with the universe so we can experience more, learn more and grow more to support our own soul growth to help us evolve further.

In our lives, moment by moment, each vibration we create attracts the same vibration toward us based on the frequency we are resonating with. The frequency is based on thoughts, beliefs, emotions and feelings. We are made up of many things. Let's co-create a new reality, living life in the new environment, filling it with honesty and truth. Each one of us is responsible to work on ourselves to raise our vibration of Oneself. At one level you are one, and at another level we are all ONE.

We are a part of Gaia and we directly contribute to the outcome of this process. We have the opportunity to help Gaia accelerate in her graduation process. With our co-creative efforts, she will need less healing and will have less pain to endure. It is the pain that mankind projects outward from being unconscious which makes the graduation process harder. Let me remind you again that every thought that the heart accepts becomes an emotion and turns into feeling. Feeling is a powerful energy that affects everything, including Gaia. The vibrations of our feelings are affecting the planetary grid.

Our vibrations either clean the energy of Gaia's body like the water in the tank or pollute it. Be more aware of the thoughts that manifest feelings that affect the energy in everything.

Help Gaia clean up the mess energetically by cleansing the negative thoughts and belief systems that are toxic and replace them with new thoughts and beliefs that are positive and loving. Be consciously aware of the power you have to make those changes. The time is now!

Kali Yuga is ending, and we want to help Gaia welcome Satya Yuga, but most importantly, we have to do what it takes and not to be left behind. We will not be left behind if we allow ourselves to accept the responsibility to co-exist within the new energy; be consciously aware and be proactively awake to make the transition and be a part of this divine process.

Get to know Oneself, the Divine presence inside each of us. What we have learned cannot be ignored. To know Oneself is to remember that we already hold the vibration of the unconditional love of Divine Source within us. Our DNA will rearrange itself, when we claim the truth of our divine power. The truth is the truth. The truth is within us. Be consciously aware of the Divine Consciousness within, it can change our body's chemistry, heal diseases, and reverse aging. Be healthy, at peace, live in love, in joy, and let's complete the ascension process as individuals and as a collective that supports Gaia in her ascension process.

The planet is ascending. Our DNA is working more efficiently than ever. Getting in touch with the seed of divine essence and wisdom will accelerate our personal and collective transformation. When we wake up to our truth and claim our true selves, our divine essence, there will no longer be conflicts within ourselves and with others. There will not be war, only peace and harmony will reign. Freewill will be honored and we will live our lives without limitations. The important choice is to choose to be in harmony with oneself, and with others and with nature, have more respect for nature. We are on the cusp of the discovery of this truth.

It is time to think outside of the box we have been placed around our consciousness. We are the ones who make the difference. We must take on spiritual mastery with the intention of a master and know how to get along and understand our human needs for collective growth. We are here to interact, to teach and learn from one another and to enhance our abilities to grow spiritually. We live in a society that sets limits on us and we cannot grow easily under those limitations. Age old accepted traditions and cultures may hold us back instead of letting us blossom. Our beautiful traditions and cultures can bring light to us if we are more accepting of one another. Our differences make us each beautiful. While we are different, one love unites us all.

After growing up in Thailand and practically living the rest of my life in the US, I can see a huge difference between the belief systems of Eastern and Western culture. I was lost in between the extreme differences for a number of years. As I described in the previous chapter, at one point I felt like I did not belong anywhere and now as I've claimed my divine light, I have respect for everyone's freewill. I completely accept all people, how they are and who they choose to be. Now, instead of feeling that I do not belong anywhere, I have a new feeling that I belong everywhere. Anywhere I choose to be! There is no separation between me and others now that I'm able to accept the differences in everyone's belief systems. I am fully aware that we are all divine sparks having human experiences and we affect one another in a grand way whether we are aware of it or not.

Remember that Gaia is being affected by our thought processes; the way we react, and handle life affects Gaia tremendously. All of our feelings become powerful energy that is stored directly in her grids. So, how about giving ourselves the gift of acceptance and stop feeling separated from one another? Although, we have different ethnic groups, traditions, cultures and belief systems, we are part of humanity which co-exist in Gaia. Cooperation is needed. We need to get along, and help one another ascend to this New Earth, the new energy that will benefit us all. Gaia will not interfere with our freewill whether we choose to ascend with her or not, but by choosing to ascend with her it will help her accelerate her ascension process more rapidly. Everybody wins in this, right? Let's do it together, shall we?

Keep working on self-love and self-acceptance because your positive vibrations from the love that you have for yourself will touch all of those who exist in your circle. Anything that you choose to do with your positive vibrations will have a positive effect on others. It is your love and joy that can help raise the vibration of others. Imagine if each one of us had already done this self-work, this beautiful world would be much more pleasant and divine.

This is how we can help cleanse the Earth of negative vibrations. The shift of consciousness from the Old Earth to the New Earth can be accelerated even further. The New Earth is peaceful; people are in harmony with one another, living life in cooperation, not in competition, in honesty and in truth. This is what the New Earth is like. This is how we can purposely recreate a new way of being on the New Earth with the vibrations of the Divine spirit existing in us.

The eternal core is always there, and it keeps incarnating into a new lifetime to learn and to grow. We have soul contracts with others and sometimes they may have to create circumstances which have us experience darkness so we can learn and grow from them and become the light that we are. It is in the divine plan that we came in with, that we just simply forgot.

To accelerate spiritual growth is to love more. Love each other much more, even the ones that give us a hard time and create disharmony within us. Especially, the ones that we have difficulty in giving love to. Forgiveness sets us free from painful grudges. Love the one you are looking at in the mirror more. The one that deserves the most unconditional love, affection, compassion, kindness, peace and joy is in the mirror looking back at you. More love is what we all need and what we all can give to ourselves and one another with the exercise of our freewill. Love heals everything. Love makes us whole again. Love is the most potent key to accelerate our spiritual evolution and to grow, evolve and ascend.

Hatred and fear will do the opposite. They will stop growth; even take us backwards, falling back into the old energy and the old belief systems that separates humanity. The old energy is rising to the surface right now. It is time for humanity to have discernment. We must have awareness to make new choices with loving kindness. Discernment allows us to raise our awareness of what needs to be changed and focus our efforts on the changes needed. Let me remind you again that we can choose love over hatred, courage over fear, harmony over disharmony, joy over sadness, compassion over anger, abundance over lack and so on. Freewill is extremely powerful. However, we must know what to choose so we can implement it to serve us for the highest purpose and the greatest good.

We are a part of One because there is only one humanity. We each experience a different taste of life. We are all of the exact same energy. We are born, we grow, we experience life and we leave the physical forms and go back to be One with Original Source Energy. We go back to a non-physical form and perhaps some of us get to do it over again, wearing different costumes, playing a new role in a totally different story in order to grow and evolve further by having a new experience. It is wisest to learn your lessons now, evolve, and live from the heart. It is an act of self-love to be present.

Having awareness is essential because every choice that we make will affect Gaia and one another. When we choose light and love, we benefit Gaia and all those around us, as well as ourselves. More people are waking up to their truth now and as a result, the awakened souls play an important role in this divine process of influencing others who are still in the awakening process. Every time the light is brightened, there will be less and less darkness. When each one of us finds our divine sparks within, we are able to emanate our divine light to the entire environment that we are in. We brighten up the whole place with the light of kindness, compassion, love and joy.

In conclusion, we need to find the ultimate knowing within ourselves and let it be the vehicle to help us ride up to the highest vibration in this ascension process with Gaia. I highly suggest that my readers read the books, "The Ancient Secret of The Flower of Life volumes I[15] and II[16]" by Drunvalo Melchizedek. These two books will help you understand how your light being is created in the physical body and that it is an ascension vehicle for this process. Learning how to increase the light within our own bodies increases our ability to use our minds to direct our ascension process.

We are in the midst of making a transition with Gaia from the old energy into the new energy. This process of conscious evolution of Gaia and mankind is an event of considerable magnitude. The whole planet is ascending into a higher vibration, a higher consciousness. Gaia has two consciousnesses now, the vibration of the old energy in the Kali

---

[15] Melchizedek, D. (1999), *The Ancient Secret of the Flower of Life, Volume 1.* Light Technology Publishing: Flagstaff.

[16] Melchizedek, D. (2001), *The Ancient Secret of the Flower of Life, Volume 2.* Light Technology Publishing: Flagstaff.

Yuga and the vibration of the new energy of the Satya Yuga, the Old Earth (3D) and the New Earth (5D). When we tune into our own heart and divinity, we access the big heart of the universe, Divine Source. Focusing on love, light, joy and heart wisdom tunes us in to the New Earth (5D) now.

Humanity is welcome to ascend with Gaia and freewill is being respected. The most important choice that we have to make is to be in alignment with the new energy. It is for us to be consciously aware of the choices between high vibrations and low vibrations. The tools have been given to and the choices available have been shown throughout this entire book. Source has offered simple abundance and emphasized LOVE; the same unconditional love that Source has for everyone.

It is the same love that already lies within us. It is pure and instantly available in every moment. The source of knowledge and the source of love are both within us and in every particle of the universe. When we tune to our inside, we feel everything outside. Love is the bridge to that connection. Claim it, own it and embody it! Love is all we need! Self-love is the most important love of all, because it opens the door to the divine! Be in the essence of love and JUST BE! Thank you for reading and thank yourself for making the highest choice to ascend with Gaia.

~Afterword from Patti, the Painting~

This section is Patti's reflection on writing this book. My entire journey has helped me progress in life beyond what I could ever have imagined. It has helped me tap into my inner-knowing, inner-guidance (intuition), and to learn to trust it too. I'm able to innerstand the feelings inside of me, and to differentiate if they are from the head or from the heart, my ego mind or my loving heart. Every thought that the heart accepts becomes an emotion that turns into a feeling. The loving heart truly has no fear, nor hatred, because it has no judgement. It flows joyously with any circumstances. The ego, on the other hand, is like muddy water. It is fearful, projecting anger from judgement, which contaminates the heart.

When I'm aware of this, it heightens my ability to discern and to know who is behind the steering wheel of my vehicle, the little self/the lower self or the bigger self/the Higher Self. I have freewill like everyone else and I choose to hand the steering wheel to my best self and navigate through my journey with loving kindness. I am better equipped to handle situations without being influenced by negative reactions. This ability alone has saved me from getting into arguments and having conflicts and disagreements with others. I now flow with the moment and I am more accepting. When I am more accepting, I have peace and harmony. This is how I stay healthy because my body does not have stress and tension to react to. The body reacts to all emotions and creates hormones and chemicals in the body's systems. I am healthy because my body releases mostly positive chemicals, such as dopamine, serotonin and endorphins supporting relaxation, peace of mind, positive habits, and a strong immune system, keeping me well. Amazingly, the magic in this has switched my life from illness to wellness; low self-esteem to high value and self-worth, lack of awareness to being fully conscious and aware of freewill, from lack of self-love to fully loving self and then naturally the love overflowing to others unconditionally. Practicing non-judgement and unconditional love has helped me with acceptance of divine light in everyone.

I'm aware that some people may dim their light and perhaps do not yet remember the value of self-love, but I trust that when they are ready to search within, they will find the hidden treasure that is there and waiting patiently to be found just like I've found mine. Like attracts like! I've formed new friendships with like spirits who are loving, kind and compassionate. We bestow positive emotion and support upon each other with honesty and enjoy our genuine relationships with one another. In my family relationships, I offer friendship to them before I play the role of spouse, mother, sister, daughter, aunt, niece, cousin or mother-in-law. We often take our family members for granted. We should place importance on nurturing friendships with our families. When we offer friendship to our family, we do not take them for granted and we give them more courtesy and consideration in all our interactions with them. People in my family are more at peace around me when they choose to be because they know that I will not judge them and I'm truly accepting of them like good friends do with one another.

Occasionally, we may create disharmony and not be able to present our true light to one another. It is good to know that this too shall pass. We can choose not to fight other people's battles and walk away silently until One's ego becomes aware of its thought forms and its actions. This is an opportunity for One to grow and thrive. On rare occasions, I, as a spouse, have to remind myself to not take things personally and find my peace of mind away from the action and wait for light to shine through. Sometimes, I observe One's ego throwing a tantrum like a two-year old towards family members, and I remind myself to stay on the observation deck. I avoid getting into battles and instead support people in getting through the situation at hand. Because we do not evolve at the same rate, it is helpful to be aware that some of us may ascend with Gaia and some may not. Source will not override our freewill. Eventually, we all will evolve back to Source with our own timing. All is well. By doing that, I've been able to avoid conflicts. Consequently, we often have more joy when we are together, especially, during our big gatherings during holidays. I have been able to create my new reality in the relationships with everyone in my circle, and that is heaven on earth for me. This reality too can be yours, if you wish. In this book, I already poured my heart out to show you how it can be done. It is as simple as it sounds. You can start in this moment by looking at yourself in the mirror, smiling and saying I love you to yourself and see what your heart feels.

Trust in Divine Source, the origin of love in each of us. We do not need to search the cosmos to find Source. Source is already within each of us as our own Higher Self. When we stop separating ourselves from Source and from one another, we will have a better innerstanding of the meaning of Oneness. We need to remember that the Higher Self in us is the same love and light of Source that is the original life force energy and frequency signal that we originated from.

The energy and consciousness within us are like a tank we use to collect water. We can collect water from anywhere and put any water we choose into our tank. The water collected becomes one combined form of liquid. Within that tank, negative emotions and thoughts are the mud that originate from the lower self, the ego mind. When we clear the mud and stop creating it, it is easier to see the clear water.

The pure water is the Higher Self. Beyond the pure water of the Higher Self is the supremely clear water of Source. We are here on Earth to collect life experiences like collecting all kinds of water and pouring it into the tank that is us. When we focus on positive thoughts and emotions, we see, hear and feel the Higher Self and Source, through the clear water.

The purpose is for Source to experience the imperfection through us as we exercise our freewill. We get to choose our experience through thoughts that our hearts accept. The Higher self is the Source within us and is having our experiences with us in every moment through the feelings that our hearts accept. We are a part of One. We are provided with all the ingredients like Alchemists who can choose any emotions to experience. If we don't like what we create, we can change it to our satisfaction.

Awareness is an important tool in this journey. Be aware of your own truth and have fun with it. As we are more aware of freewill and choose to collect clean water (positive thinking in loving kindness), the tank becomes free from murky water. We can have more fun in life and be able to make a difference in every step we take by being an example of purity at the heart level. The heart is all about love, and love gives light. Where there is light, there is no darkness. I am now more connected with the Higher Self and Source because I choose it without any resistance to be doing so. The choice is ours! Choose well and trust the process. So much love to all (you, me, Gaia and everyone).

Trust the universe! When we are in alignment with the universe, the UNI will take partnership with the VERSE. Everything will be provided for us. It always has been. I have a beautiful story to share with you. This story will demonstrate how the universe will always be ready to provide everything when we are ready to move forward.

I was still in the process of writing this book and was guided by Source under my surrogate session that Scot Holliday would be the most suitable person to give me the support in writing this book. I was delighted and was planning to reach out to him. I did not realize that the universe already set up the connection between us. Within that same week, I received Scot's most recent book (he has published 12 books and articles[17]) delivered to me from Amazon. He ordered his own book and sent it to me as a gift, "Walking Through the Door: Teaching of How to Listen to the Heart and Let the Heart Lead[18]". I was extremely happy as I was acknowledged the synchronicity of that.

---

[17] List of publications www.changetacticsllc.com/publications
[18] Holliday, S. (2019), *Walking Through the Door: Teachings of How to Listen to the Heart and Let the Heart Lead.* Change

I enjoyed it so much that I finished reading it in one day. I thanked him and let him know that I too was writing a book for Source and was told that he would be the perfect one to help me with it. He graciously accepted my offer to contribute to this book and I felt the need to put as much focus and drive as possible into finishing it (I was biding my time prior to that). It was indeed a Divine plan. Scot, the professor, was not teaching that semester. He was taking on a research project and had time to help me with my book. He applied the entirety of his heart and soul, one thousand percent drive and love into it. His heart was fully open, and his vibration was raised through the process.

The raising of his vibration improved his family dynamics. His family's vibration started to shift with him. I love and appreciate how he has a beautiful way of bringing the painting to life. He does a beautiful job framing this artwork. I'm grateful for the beautiful experience of working with him. On the following pages is what he has to say in his own words. In loving gratitude, ~Patti

Tactics LLC: Washington, D.C. Available on amazon in hard and soft format https://amzn.to/35DB1s4

~Afterword from Scot, the Framer~

Note from my heart to the readers of this book, my family and Patti. When Patti invited me to edit this book, I thought she was inviting me to proofread the grammar and polish the use of metaphor and language. What she was really inviting me to do was see the universe through the eyes of her heart. Patti walks the talk. She does live with a joyful heart every day. She does this so that she can live in a vibration of the new earth, which is of joy, love, peace and harmony. She also does this so that she can hold this space, frequency and vibration for others.

After being able to play in this space with her for several months, I now realize I can live in this space too and that I am already at home in it. In this book Patti is the painting. She is inviting you into the painting and you can become part of this painting with her. This book is a portal to another dimension, to another frequency, to that of the 5D earth.

As I was reading, editing and re-reading this book over the past several months, I felt my overall emotions and thought patterns lighten up and become more loving and joyful. I let go of subtle anxiety and melancholy that was making me feel sluggish. I felt more comfortable helping family members connect with one another and make peace with each other. I became more comfortable holding a higher frequency heart space for myself, my family and all those around me. I noticed recently I was really able to listen to others from the vantage of my heart and speak from my heart. When I do that it feels as if my mouth and ears are located on my heart rather than my head.

I notice when I interact with life with a heart focus, rather than a mind and ego focus, everything flows better, is more harmonious and joyful. Difficult moments in conversations are no longer stressful, they just flow. Little problems that arise during the day, seem to work themselves out with ease, rather than being difficult. Flowing between working on the computer, listening to family members tell their stories, exercising, driving on an errand, solving a problem, meditating, and just listening; becomes easy.

When I connect with life using a focus on the heart and on love, the same flow and harmony within me, begins to occur outside of me. When we maintain the flow of love inside, we are able to find the flow of love outside of ourselves more easily, and help others do the same. The following paragraph is what being in the flow of love feels like to me. Sending everyone love and kindness.

To become part of the frequency of 5D earth, of love, all you have to do is claim it and be it. Just feel your own desire to do it and become it. There is no technique needed. All that is needed is your agreement. You make that agreement using your mind and heart together. The mind is the rudder that directs the ship of your heart and your soul into this alignment. It is like pushing a boat away from the dock, letting it drift into the current, and then letting that current carry you. Your mind is what gives you that push away from the dock. Your heart is what guides you in the right direction. The current is the love of source and the love of the universe flowing everywhere. Let go of the security of the port, of the dock and let yourself be carried by the currents of love. Let yourself flow with love. Let yourself be love. ~Scot

Dr. Scot Holliday, The Editor,

Life Coach, CHWC, Writer, Organizational Change Consultant at Change Tactics LLC, and Professor at GWU and UMD, for more information see www.changetacticsllc.com

~About the Author~

Patti Intoranat is a Certified Hypnotherapist, Soul Coach, Writer and Radio Talk Show host. She is intuitive. She has a gift of being clairaudient. She received guidance from the Higher wisdom of Divine Source on how to help herself and others. She serves others by sharing direct wisdom from Source and wisdom her own heart has learned on her journey of self-discovery, healing and spiritual connection. Patti has had a successful career as a Level Three Quantum Healing Hypnosis Practitioner, the most prestigious level within the QHHT program established by Dolores Cannon and was personally trained by the great master.

Patti received guidance from Source to write this book based on her own personal journey. The stories describe how she was knocking at death's door with a terminal illness and how she overcame her challenges, leading her to become a spiritual teacher. She shows others how to find love and light within themselves. She practices what she teaches and has over a thousand success stories to teach and inspire others with. For more information see ***www.hypnosisphenomenon.com***

~Glossary~

This section provides definitions for key words used in this book. Any word in a language can defined in more than one way. We share definitions in this section that relates to the lessons this book intends to share.

3D Earth: The energy of the third dimensional earth, the old earth. This represents control, sense of lack, greed, ego focus, and lack of disconnection with love, the Higher Self, Source and Gaia. We are in 3D Earth to experience human imperfection and learn to evolve and ascend energetically to the 5D Earth.

5D Earth: The energy of the fifth dimensional earth, the new earth. This represents people living in harmony with one-self and one another, all living beings, Gaia and Source. Its frequency represents love, unconditional love, the right brain, the Higher Self, Source and ascension.

Akashic Records: An enormous record of all experiences of our planet and the people in it. It can be personalized to the unique record of one person and it contains the record of the person on every moment and in every lifetime that the person is living and has lived.

Alpha Brainwave State: The first altered state of consciousness. Bridges the gap between

our conscious thinking and subconscious mind.
Promotes deep relaxation, peace and harmony.
Activates the pineal gland and the right brain.
Associated with meditation, being creative,
being in nature, and art. A source of deep
wisdom. When we meditate, it has been
scientifically proven that our brainwaves slow
down to the Alpha Brainwave state, becoming
slower and deeper than the Beta Brainwave
state. In this state, we tap into the pineal gland
and activate the right side of the brain. We
reconnect and stay connected with the
collective consciousness while our brainwaves
are in Alpha level of consciousness.

Ascension: The shift of consciousness from
being focused on the ego (human self) to being
focused on unconditional love (the soul, Higher
Self and Source).

Aura: The energy field around every being
including people, plants, minerals and others.
A person who can see the aura is referred to as
being clairvoyant. Some people have an ability
to see auras. Seeing auras is a skill and
consciousness that can be learned.

Awareness: This is what a person puts their
attention on and focuses their consciousness
toward and recognizes as distinct. There are a
broad range of ways the word is used.
Practicing meditation is a natural way to raise
our awareness and raise our ability to have
discernment of our thought processes. Once we

become aware of a thought, belief, emotion or feeling we can then reject, accept or change it. We can be aware every moment of our lives if we choose to be.

Being: This is a big focus of this book. We can simply choose to be at a frequency we desire and live in that vibration. For example, one does not need to study for years on how to be loving, one can just choose to vibrate at the frequency of love and be love. We will get to do less and BE more when we practice Beingness.

Beta Brainwave State: Alert, conscious, intellectual focus. Left brain focused. Lower consciousness of the mind. Connected to the ego. This frequency is related to negative emotions and thoughts, causing stress and fear. This is also where critical thinking, planning and problem solving resides.

Clairaudient: The ability to perceive energy as sound. Patti has a natural ability to hear lifeforce energy. This is how she describes it, *"I described my gift of being clairaudient earlier as, I hear frequency and interpret vibration. I translate it into feeling and vibrate it into an image and language in the physical realm. I operate as an empath, as a vibration-ship to others that I work with. I serve as a conduit for their frequency."*

Collective Consciousness: This usually refers to the shared consciousness of all beings

271

on Earth. We can consciously connect to the collective consciousness through unconditional love and we realize we all share one large energy field; we are all one.

Consciousness: This is what we are each individually aware of. As we learn, grow and glow our consciousness expands and we can perceive more of reality, our thoughts, our beliefs, our emotions and our feelings. It is important to become more conscious every day and increase our ability to discern truth and be unconditionally loving.

Delta Brainwave State: Deepest level of relaxation and restoration. Deepest level of sleep and rejuvenation.

Dharmakaya Vipassana Meditation (DVM): A Buddhist meditation method focusing on seeing the nature of oneself and the universe clearly.

Divine Source: The original life force energy of unconditional love that is the origin of everything, everywhere.

Dolores Cannon: Dolores devoted over 50 years of her life to serving others as a teacher, past life regression practitioner, psychic researcher, and an international speaker who lectured on all the continents of the world. Her books are translated into over twenty languages. She spoke to radio and television audiences worldwide. Articles about and by Dolores appeared in several U.S. and international magazines and newspapers. Dolores received the "Orpheus Award" in Bulgaria, for highest advancement in the research of psychic phenomenon. She received Outstanding contribution and Lifetime Achievement awards from several hypnosis organizations. She was the founder of Quantum Healing Hypnosis Technique (QHHT). She wrote 20 books and created dozens of videos (available on YouTube). She taught about unconditional love, past life regressions, Christ, healing, consciousness, our connection to the cosmos and other spiritual topics. She was Patti's teacher.

Dopamine: Positive brain chemical. Provides a short-term happy feeling. Can relate to good or bad habit formation.

Endorphins: Positive brain chemical. Is a natural painkiller. Are released in response to pain. Creates the feeling of a "runner's high".

Evolve: To return to love. We are all growing and learning at our own pace. We all eventually learn our nature is love and come to know it consciously.

Freewill: A gift from Source. Our divine right to choose. We can choose what we want to think, and even Source will not interfere with what we choose to think. We can choose to liberate ourselves from limiting and controlling beliefs, and live in joy, love and peace every day.

Four Chemicals Produced by Positive Thought & Emotion: When we think good thoughts that our heart accepts, they turn into positive emotion, the body starts reacting and releases organic, positive chemicals. These positive chemicals are dopamine, oxytocin, serotonin, and endorphins.

Gaia: The name for the new 5D earth resonating at the frequency of unconditional love. It is the spiritual name for the earth and implies she has a feminine nature. She is a conscious being, a sentient being, and she resonates at the frequency of unconditional love.

Higher Self: The Divine spirit of our souls. Our individual bridge to Source. The nature of the Higher Self and Source are the same, of unconditional love and all wisdom. The personal connection we perceive with Source is the Higher Self.

Innerstand: To deeply understand something with our heart and mind.

Left brain: Our intellectual side. Logical thinking, critical thinking, problem solving. The conscious mind associated with the ego (lower self).

Life Coach: A person who supports another person to become the best version of her/himself. Coaches support individuals to create their own goals, a path to achieve them and self-empowerment. The focus is on empowering the client. For more information on how Scot approaches Life Coaching see www.changetacticsllc.com/life-coaching

Love: Love is the invisible energy that connects every molecule in the universe. Love is the energy of the Higher Self, Source, the spirit, the soul and God. In the movie Star Wars, the force is love. Love is not something we have, it is something all around us that flows through us, in us and is us. You are love and are surrounded by love. Love gives light and where there is light, there is no darkness. Love is so perfect. Love heals.

Meditation: This is a powerful practice for quieting the lower conscious mind of the left brain, where the ego expresses its mental chatter. It will bring you into the alpha wave brain state, promoting awareness, consciousness, healing, rejuvenation, and relaxation. The benefits are countless. Practicing daily meditation helps us reconnect and stay connected with our Higher Selves.

A guided meditation from the book:

1. Close your eyes and place hands on your heart.

2. Take a few deep breaths and imagine that you are breathing through your heart. You are getting in touch with your loving heart, the Source within you.

3. Place your focus within and listen to the frequency inside your brain. Notice the sound and feeling.

4. Focus on the frequency (sound and/or feeling) and turn up the volume. Let yourself hear or feel it more fully. You are getting in touch with the original life force of the frequency signal within you.

5. Allow your breath to slow down and naturally deepen as you relax. Allow your mouth to open slightly, if it helps you go deeper into relaxation. Focus within and follow your breathing. Be aware of your breath as you are breathing in and breathing out. You are getting in touch with the life force energy that is in everything and is in you as you draw in and release your breathe.

6. Be in silent mode. Don't think, just listen to the sound of the frequency or the silence. Feel the connection that you are having with your loving heart/Source in you. Be receptive. If you notice yourself thinking let the mind relax and just listen. Listening to your wisdom rather than thinking is the key. Yare in the alpha state, once you are listening. Stay in this state of listening and receiving as long as needed. This is a great foundational daily meditation practice.

7. Another step you can add to your foundational practice if it is comfortable is listening to your heartbeat. Then you can choose to listen to your breath, heartbeat, frequency or a combination of them. Remember to listen, rather than think or do.

Neutrinos: The term from quantum physics for energy that makes up the entire universe from the smallest to the largest thing. Energy is everywhere, in every being and everything. Neutrinos are the same as chi, prana and life force energy. They are also referred to as God Particles.

New Earth: Is a concept found in over 35 religious and spiritual traditions. The New Earth refers to living at the consciousness of love, where we choose love, joy, peace, gratitude and happiness every day. It is a frequency of being we can choose to tune into and live at. It is the energy of Gaia. It is the energy of 5D.

Non-Judgement: Being accepting of others whether we agree or disagree with them. This is what allows us to embrace unconditional love. This is key to personal and collective evolution. Non-judgement is the principle that allows us to master the crafts of: (1) unconditional love, (2) compassion, (3) acceptance, (4) forgiveness and (5) trust.

Oxytocin: Positive brain chemical. Creates trust and a loving feeling. Is often called the hugging drug, due to its release during physical contact with others.

Past Life Regression: Connecting to your past lives in a meditative or hypnotic state so that you can clear trauma, learn life lessons and reclaim your spiritual gifts. It helps you remember who you are. This is part of the focus of the Quantum Healing Hypnosis Technique (QHHT), that Patti specializes in.

Qigong: A Chinese method of being in touch with life force energy in a form of moving meditation. One can use the practice to increase one's ability to move chi in the energy field and body, heal illness, clear and focus the mind, martial arts training and other areas. Qigong works well as a compliment to other practices including meditation, energy/light work and traditional physical exercise.

Quantum Healing Hypnosis Technique (QHHT): QHHT is a method for connecting to the Higher Self in a hypnotic state created by Dolores Cannon. This technique has been proven to be effective on thousands of people all over the world regardless of their age, gender, personality, religious beliefs or cultural backgrounds. The method helps the client to connect to a state of collective consciousness. While in the hypnotic state you have the opportunity to make a deep connection to the Higher Self, connect to other lives to receive answers to your questions and self-healing. Often, we have negative thoughts, beliefs, emotions and feelings that prevent us from becoming the best version of ourselves. Connecting to the Higher Self can empower oneself to become present and choose positive thoughts, beliefs, emotions and feelings. Adopting a positive way of being is the bridge to love, happiness and joy. QHHT was founded by Dolores Cannon. Patti is a Level Three Quantum Healing Hypnosis Practitioner and was one of the first six practitioners personally trained and approved by Dolores to practice QHHT.

Quantum: This refers to the smallest realm perceptible by science, 100 nanometers (10^{-9} meters). It is a term from Quantum Physics. This is new area of science that is creating new theories about how the largest things in the universe (galaxies) and the smallest things (nano particles and neutrinos) operate as one.

Right brain: The intelligence side. Intuition, wisdom, creativity, collective consciousness of subconscious, super conscious and supreme consciousness. Associated with the soul (Higher Self).

Selfness: Many people have a misperception about self-love and forget and deny themselves love. When we are selfness; we focus on being wholesome, we have 100 percent to give and are complete.   Selfness is a balance between Selfish and Selfless. Selfish means someone who thinks of themselves first, second and last. Selfless means someone who thinks of others first, second and last. There is no balance there. When we think of ourselves and take care of ourselves first and become wholesome, we will be able to flow our wholeness to others naturally.   This way we can be of service to others more effectively and successfully. Selfness is the bridge to self-love. Self-love is the bridge to unconditional love, the Higher Self and Source.

Serotonin: Positive brain chemical. Related to a feeling of accomplishment or recognition. It is even believed to affect digestion, bone growth and organ development.

Soul Coach: Someone who aids people in connecting to their Higher Self. Teaches people how to stay integrated and stay connected with Source at the soul level and align to their life highest potential in life. Patti does soul coaching with clients who need support in the ascension process at any time, including before or after QHHT. For information on how Patti approaches soul coaching see www.hypnosisphenomenon.com

Source: Short name for Divine Source. Source is unconditional love, all knowledge and all wisdom. The energy that everything in every universe originates from is Source. Source is an infinite energy of unconditional love and people may call Source by many other names such as God, the Creator, Yahweh, Supreme Being, All mighty, All that is, Love, Light, Oneness, The infinite, Oversoul and The Higher Self.

Stress Hormones: What we create within our bodies when we perceive something as stressful. They include adrenaline, noradrenaline (fight or flight) and cortisol. These hormones destroy the healthy cells in the body and can lead to disease, depending on the vulnerability of a person's body and severity of the stress. This is how we make ourselves sick. The stress hormones are created as a reaction to negative emotion. Stress hormones store in cellular memory and turn into emotional baggage.   We can learn to stop triggering them by becoming aware of our own thoughts and emotions, and choose to be loving, happy, joyful, and peaceful.

Sun Gazing: The practice of looking at the sun during the first or last hour of the day when the sun's rays are less direct. It can be an energizing and clearing practice that raises one's vibration and reduces stress. There are many videos on YouTube describing how to begin this practice on your own if it resonates with you.

Surrogate Session: Connecting with a person's Higher Self through another person as a surrogate subject under hypnosis. This is done in Enhanced Quantum Healing sessions when the person of focus is not able to be physically present or is unable to get into a receptive brain state for QHHT.

Synchronicity: Source in action anonymously. Coincidence that is not mere coincidence. An occurrence being synchronized by the universe in perfect timing.

Theta Brainwave State: Deep state of consciousness. Deep connection to innate knowing.

Unconditional Love: The Divine Love that is pure and perfect. The Divine Being, the origin of us and everything, that created the universe and is unconditional love. We are a part of the Divine sparks that are unconditional love. We come from unconditional love. Learning self-love opens the door to the Divine Love that is unconditional. Being in a state of non-judgment is the bridge to unconditional love.

Vibrationship: A person who becomes a conduit to the frequency of the vibration of Divine Source and downloads the information from vibrations of the Source of knowledge and translates it into a language in the physical realm.

Namaste

·

Made in the USA
Middletown, DE
17 July 2022

69569964R00175